A GUIDE TO THE HISTORIC

SHOPS & RESTAURANTS

OF NEW ORLEANS

✦

A Guide to the Historic
Shops & Restaurants
of New Orleans

THE LITTLE BOOKROOM ✦ NEW YORK

© 2004 The Little Bookroom
Design: Louise Fili Ltd.
Cover: Vintage postcard of Old Absinthe House,
collection of the publisher.

Library of Congress Cataloging-in-Publication Data
A guide to the historic shops & restaurants of New Orleans.– 1st ed. p. cm. ISBN 1-892145-27-8
1. Restaurants–Louisiana–New Orleans. 2. Stores, Retail–Louisiana–New Orleans.
TX907.3.L82N4354 2004 647.95763'65--dc22 2004001772

First printing July 2004
Printed in China by P. Chan & Edward, Inc. All rights reserved, which
includes the right to reproduce this book or portions thereof in any form whatsoever.

Photo captions on p. 186

The Little Bookroom
1755 Broadway, Fifth floor
New York, NY 10019
(212) 293-1643; (212) 333-5374 fax
editorial@littlebookroom.com
www.littlebookroom.com

Distributed by Publishers Group West;
in the UK by Macmillan Distribution Ltd.

Contents

✦

Introduction

I F YOU DO NOT LIVE IN NEW ORLEANS, YOU MAY BE TEMPTED TO ASK SOMEONE WHO DOES WHY NO ONE EVER BOTHERS TO UNTANGLE THE WEATHERED MARDI Gras beads from the live oak limbs along St. Charles Avenue, why so many of the city's faltering buildings go undemolished, or why people still flock to that tavern where the counters sag and cobwebs trail from the ceiling like veils of Spanish moss. Ask any New Orleanian these things, and he will look at you as though you've lost your mind.

One of the city's virtues is its casual comfort with its past. In New Orleans, history is no brittle, disused heirloom, but a vibrant part of the city, continually revived and nourished in the daily lives of the people who live here: people who go for drinks at the same taverns that their great-grandparents frequented, who take a watch in for repairs at the jewelry store where an ancestor purchased it a century ago, who work in the restaurants their families started when they first arrived from abroad.

The shops, restaurants, and other businesses whose stories this book tells — places that have been here for three quarters of a century or more — are as vital to the city's image of itself as any of the sights that typically grace the postcard racks. The histories of these old enterprises, which range from New Orleans's proudest dining establishments to the neighborhood locksmith shop, are the stories of the people who immigrated here, from Europe, Nova Scotia, the Caribbean, and elsewhere, in pursuit of better lives in a new country; yet when they arrived, they found a city whose passions bore an uncommon resemblance to the worlds they'd left behind. The newcomers carried with them the spirit of thrift, hard work, and enterprise that might have made New Orleans into a southern Chicago or New York, but in the Crescent City, they soon discovered that ambition generally takes a backseat to more dearly held philosophies — that no meal can be too big or last too long, and that there's a simple human wisdom in knocking a week off of work each spring to drink cocktails in excess and watch parades go by.

Visitors can experience old New Orleans with very little effort, within the walls of these old businesses. Some of the places listed in this guide boast grand pasts and famous patrons, but it could be argued that the true character of the city lies not in the more spectacular episodes of its local lore — Andrew Jackson's victory the British in the Battle of New Orleans, the birth of jazz in the brothels and saloons of Storyville, the schemings and impieties of Earl and Huey Long — but in the subtler, more humble spectacles that endure in these establishments: the well-mannered hubbub of a Friday afternoon in Galatoire's, the smoke-stained timbers in Lafitte's Blacksmith Shop, the fluorescent glare of Casamento's restaurant, the noble mahogany gloom of The Columns Hotel, the broken soda fountain at Royal Pharmacy, the starched table linens at Antoine's, or the bare tabletops at Bozo's, where the menus are just as they were yesterday and just as they will be tomorrow.

FOOD
AND
DRINK

Acme Oyster House

SOON AFTER HIS INAUGURATION AS THE MAYOR OF NEW YORK CITY IN 1933, FIORELLO LAGUARDIA APPEARED IN A NEWSREEL SMASHING A SLOT MACHINE with a sledgehammer. The slot machine, along with a thousand others like it, belonged to mobster Frank Costello, who was suddenly in a hurry to relocate his gaming business to a more accommodating town. New Orleans seemed like a good bet. Louisiana Governor Huey Long agreed, and soon Costello's fleet of one-armed bandits was en route to the Crescent City.

Costello placed his slot machines in bars and juke joints throughout New Orleans with the help of James "Diamond Jim" Moran, an ex-boxer and former bodyguard to Huey Long. Moran's underworld connections were well-known (he served as a go-between in business deals between Long and Al Capone), though as the century wore on, Moran came to be known almost as widely for the restaurants he owned around town as for his shadowy associations.

In 1960, Moran bought the Acme Oyster House, a raucous seafood joint on Iberville Street, favored by working-class locals and sailors on furlough. The Acme Café had opened shop half a century earlier, at 117 Royal Street beside the Cosmopolitan Hotel, with a bare-bones menu of oysters and Jax and Dixie beers. In 1924, a disastrous fire razed the café, which soon reopened on Iberville as the Acme Oyster House. At the new location, Acme's menu broadened to include a roster of hot, deli-style dishes, and most afternoons the place was thronged with a population of devoted regulars. Diamond Jim, however, didn't do much good for the place. With other restaurants to attend to around town, and with Acme suffering from disastrously unrigorous bookeeping, Moran sold the oyster house in 1985 to restaurateur Mike Rodrigue. At the time the restaurant changed hands, Acme's staff was down to only one waitress and a single shucker; it was closed most afternoons by four o'clock. But even after Diamond Jim had handed over the key, he had a habit of showing up at the restaurant on short notice with a crowd of out-of-town associates, a cadre of waiters in black-tie, and enough silverware and starched table linens to impose a strange, contrived resplendence on Acme's unassuming dining room.

Over the years, Acme's atmosphere of cozy disorder has been maintained, or at least allowed to flourish unimpeded. The dining room, with its unsubtle aroma of eight decades of seafood grease and atomized crab boil, its mosaic floor of fractured brick, and its cheery discord of mismatched chandeliers conveys a feeling of comfortable chaos. The owners have retained Acme's lovely marble-topped oyster bar, and there's still enough old wood paneling here to counterbalance an abundance of neon beer signage.

Acme's specialty is, naturally, oysters, plucked from beds in Black Bay or American Bay, both in Plaquemines Parish, where the estuary waters make for salty but mild oyster flesh. One of Acme's senior shuckers, Michael "Hollywood" Broadway, is the city's third speediest oyster shucker, and can husk a dozen in sixty-seven seconds. The skin on his palms is the texture of thick canvas and is crazed with old wounds. "I'm not trying to impress anyone," he said. "I just try to keep 'em coming, clean and cold."

Aside from oysters on the half-shell, the menu also offers the usual index of New Orleans dishes: gumbo, red beans and rice, jambalaya, po' boy sandwiches, and several varieties of seafood cloaked in a crunchy, golden crust of deep-fried cornmeal.

TIMOTHY GOUJON, V.O.N.O.*

(Vendor of Oysters in New Orleans)

"To sell such [oysters], is the business and daily care of those called, in common language, oystermen — the French style them écaille….It was to this enterprising portion of the body politic that Timothy Goujon belonged. Long had he lived and labored in the cause of science, for he was a practical naturalist — perhaps you may say a conchologist — spending his days and his nights among shell-fish…We have heard that a year or two ago he involved himself in the rent of a small box of a corner shop, where his beautiful triangular lantern, covered with red worsted, and bearing the inviting inscription of 'Always Oysters, fryd, rost & in the shel,' hung out by night as a point of local attraction to the hungry and wayfaring…This speculation did not succeed, and Timothy sold out his stock in trade, including the beautiful red worsted emblem of gastronomy, and betook himself independently to the levee, like a gentleman, where he might breathe a purer air, and give exercise to his lungs, at the same time vending viva voce the inanimate quadrupeds which lay piled up with so much sang froid in his boat beside him.

"Often, of a Sunday morning, we have heard the melodious, guttural voice of Timothy Goujon, in that place in the city of New Orleans where men and women do, at this especial hour of the week, 'most congregete,' namely, in the Market-place. There have we seen and heard the sentimental Goujon trill forth harmonious ditty in accents somewhat like the following, though it would require a mixture of the French horn and the bassoon to grunt out the strain with any degree of exactness, especially the chorus: 'Ah-h-h-h-h-h-h-h-h a bonne marché — so cheep as navair vas — toutes frais — var fresh. Ah-h-h un véritable collection — jentlemens and plack folks. Ah-h-h come and puy de veritable poisson de la mer — de bonne huitres — Ah-h-h-h-h-h-h-h!'"

FROM *The New Orleans Daily Crescent*, APRIL 4, 1848

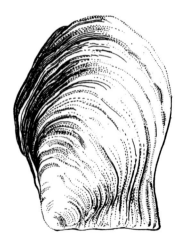

Angelo Brocato's Italian Ice Cream & Pastries

214 NORTH CARROLLTON AVENUE

between Bienville & Iberville Streets

SUNDAY-THURSDAY 9:30AM-10PM

FRIDAY-SATURDAY 9:30AM-10:30PM

☎ 504-486-0078

MANY OF THE ITALIANS WHO CAME TO LOUISIANA IN THE LATE 1800s TO CHOP SUGAR CANE WOULD CUT A SEASON'S WORTH AND THEN MAKE THE VOYAGE back across the Atlantic to their families in Italy. But Angelo Brocato stayed on, and in 1905, when he'd saved enough of his wages from the sugar fields, Brocato, rather fittingly, used the money to open a sweet shop on Ursulines Street in the French Quarter.

Brocato made his confections literally by hand. His shop wasn't equipped with a hand-cranking ice cream churn, and Brocato spent long hours laboriously churning the chilled cream, eggs, and sugar with the broad side of a wide-bladed knife. The wine Brocato used in his cannoli shells he also made himself, and during Prohibition, a meddling neighbor told the cops that Brocato was moonlighting as a bootlegger. When the police arrived, Brocato grudgingly fessed up, but what was he supposed to use for his pastries, water? Vinegar? The officers, who had perhaps tasted his cannolis, agreed, and let him off the hook.

The back end of the French Quarter, where Brocato had his shop, was a dangerous place in the early twentieth century. Rival gangs of Sicilian mobsters often battled in the narrow, cobbled streets. Angelo's son, Roy Brocato, who still works in the shop today, recalls a day when a man sprinted up Ursulines Street and jumped into a wooden barrel in front of the shop to escape a barrage of assassin's bullets.

Even the young men who weren't outright criminals could be troublesome and loutish, which posed a challenge for a merchant trying to run a civilized shop. So Angelo Brocato built two entrances to his store: one anyone could use; the other was reserved for unescorted women to come and enjoy a cool treat without being molested by the local hooliganry.

As the years passed, the store's circumstances worsened. The Depression, followed not long after by wartime rationing of milk and sugar, landed Brocato's on hard times. By the time of Angelo Brocato's death, in 1946, the Italians who'd been the shop's reliable customers were moving out of the French Quarter to Mid-City and to more distant suburban reaches. In the 1970s, current proprietor Arthur Brocato, Angelo's grandson, followed suit, and opened an attractive shop at 214 N. Carrollton Avenue. Its twisted wire chairs, faux marble tables, and stately bronze espresso machine maintain the old shop's feel. Today, Arthur Brocato and his wife Jolie sell cakes, cookies, and cannolis, as well as spumoni and gelati in shrill, delicious hues.

Antoine's Restaurant

IN 1837, FRANCE'S FIRST RAILROAD WAS MAKING ITS INAUGURAL RUN, A SHORT TRIP FROM PARIS TO ST.-GERMAIN-EN-LAYE, AND CITIZEN KING LOUIS PHILIPPE commissioned his chef Collinet to prepare a banquet for the train's arrival. Collinet knew the king liked potatoes sliced thin and fried to a crisp, and he timed the meal perfectly, lifting the potatoes from the hot oil just as the train was pulling into the station. The chef, however, was chagrined to learn that the king would be arriving later, by carriage. When the king showed up at last, Collinet plunged the already-fried potatoes into the boiling oil once more. To his astonishment, the potatoes puffed up like balloons. He called them "soufflées." They were crisp and airy, and the king was delighted with them.

Collinet confided the secret to a few close friends, one of them Antoine Alciatore, who was then chef of the Hotel de Noailles in Marseilles. When Alciatore moved to New Orleans three years later to open his restaurant, he featured Collinet's pommes de terre soufflées, prepared the same way as they are today.

Founded in 1840, Antoine's is only three years younger than New York's Delmonico's, the oldest restaurant in America. Many waiters here have served tenures in excess of fifty years, waiting at the tables of Antoine's distinguished guests. Beyond its two main dining rooms, Antoine's has a gallery of private parlors. The Carnival krewes Rex, Proteus, and Twelfth Night all have rooms named for them, where they gather to carouse and plan the year's parades. The far wall of the President's Room hides a secret door that opens on to a smaller, red-walled chamber called the Mystery Room. During Prohibition, Antoine's stopped serving liquor in the main dining room, but those in the know would duck out to the Mystery Room mid-meal (either through the President's Room, or through a second hidden portal in the ladies' lavatory) for a glass of contraband. When the drinkers returned, intoxicated, their uninformed fellow patrons would ask where they'd come across the booze. The secret room's habitués gave a single cryptic response: "It's a mystery."

Antoine's still serves the same French-Creole cuisine on which Antoine Alciatore built his reputation. Specialties include Pompano en Papillote (filet of pompano baked in a parchment bag), Poulet bonne femme (chicken sautéed and browned with potatoes, onions, garlic, and bacon), Châteaubriand, Noisettes d'agneau Alciatore (medallions of lamb wrapped in bacon, broiled, and served with béarnaise sauce on a slice of grilled pineapple), the potato soufflées, and Oysters Rockefeller, invented by Jules Alciatore in 1899, so named because of the richness of the sauce, for America's wealthiest family at the time. For dessert, try the Baked Alaska, along with a glass of the Café Brûlot, spiced brandied coffee set afire and ladled tableside in a spectacle of violet flames.

> *"She had heard it said that the proprietor, Roy Alciatore, had been offered untold sums to open branches elsewhere, and that he had proudly replied, 'there can only be one Antoine's.' She understood what he meant."*
>
> FRANCES PARKINSON KEYES, *Dinner at Antoine's*, 1948

"New Orleans, in spring-time—just when the orchards were flushing over with peach-blossoms, and the sweet herbs came to flavour the juleps—seemed to me the city of the world where you can eat and drink the most and suffer the least. ...At that comfortable tavern on Pontchartrain we had a bouillabaisse than which a better was never eaten at Marseilles..."

WILLIAM MAKEPEACE THACKERAY

Roundabout Papers, 1862

Arnaud's

between Bourbon & Dauphine Streets

MONDAY-THURSDAY 11:30AM-2:30PM, 6PM-10PM

FRIDAY-SATURDAY 11:30AM-2:30PM, 6PM-10:30PM

SUNDAY 10AM-2:30PM

☎ 504-523-5433

"THE COUNT IS GONE," A JOURNALIST STATED GRAVELY ON THE OCCASION OF ARNAUD CAZENAVE'S PASSING IN MAY OF 1948. COUNT ARNAUD, A FRENCH-born wine merchant, had no authentic claim to his title, but his legendary French Quarter restaurant, and his reputation as one of New Orleans's more notorious *bon vivants*, justified the pretension.

Cazenave declared on his menu's back flap that "A dinner chosen according to one's needs, tastes, and moods, well prepared and well served, is a joy to all senses and an impelling incentive to sound sleep, good health and long life." Cazenave put this philosophy into steady practice, spending long hours at table each night. Each morning, after fortifying himself with a split of champagne, he patrolled the restaurant with a liver-pummeling cup of "half-and-half" — half coffee and half bourbon — of which he'd drink twenty cups by the end of the day. A doctor who didn't have much faith in Cazenave's self-prescribed elixir suggested that the Count switch to orange juice. "Not too bad once you get used to it," he conceded grudgingly, and lived another eleven years, to the respectable age of seventy-two.

Arnaud's, which opened in 1918, wasn't long in becoming one of the city's best-regarded restaurants, and the premises expanded with its reputation. The Count bought up the adjoining properties, displacing an opium den and a bordello, making Arnaud's the French Quarter's largest restaurant.

After the Count's death, the sprawling complex passed to his daughter Germaine Cazenave Wells. Her appetites for food, drink, and celebration rivaled the Count's, and Germaine reigned as queen in a record-breaking twenty-two Carnival balls. Germaine also established a parade of her own, held every Easter Sunday, whose unofficial purpose was to showcase her latest extravagant hat. A gallery upstairs houses Germaine's mammoth collection of headware, as well as gowns and finery from six decades of carnival balls.

By 1978, Arnaud's had fallen into disrepair and almost all of its many dining rooms had long been closed. Germaine Wells sold the restaurant to hotelier Archie Casbarian, who undertook an extensive, though graceful, renovation. The main dining room, a pavilion of fluted metal columns, chandeliers, and beveled glass, is an elegant study in Jazz Age splendor.

Today, the menu still offers traditional haute Creole cuisine, with occasional contemporary innovations. Specialties include Shrimp Arnaud, smoked pompano, oysters Bienville, crisp Brabant potatoes, oyster bisque, crawfish O'Connor (brandy-flamed in lobster sauce), Creole crabcakes, pompano en croûte (grilled pompano and scallop mousse in puff pastry), trout meunière, roast quail with foie gras, veal tournedos in wild mushroom sauce, filet mignon with mushroom and béarnaise sauces, as well as other Creole standards.

For casual dining, visit Arnaud's Remoulade, the restaurant's offshoot café next door on Bourbon Street.

ONE POUND
NET WEIGHT.
FRENCH RESTAURANT
REGISTERED.
BRAND
ROASTED
COFFEE AND CHICORY.
IMPORTERS COFFEE CO.
LIMITED
NEW ORLEANS, LOUISIANA.

Bozo's Seafood House

3117 21ST STREET

between Causeway Boulevard & Ridgelake Drive

TUESDAY-THURSDAY 11AM-3PM, 5-10PM

FRIDAY-SATURDAY 11AM-3PM, 5-11PM

☎ 504-831-8666

MOST RESTAURANTS AS OLD AS BOZO'S SEAFOOD HOUSE HAVE PASSED TO THIRD OR FOURTH GENERATIONS OF FAMILY OWNERSHIP, BUT BOZO'S HAS changed hands only once, from Chris "Bozo" Vodonavich the First to Chris "Bozo" Vodonavich the Second, who has been working in the kitchen here for over half a century. Bozo's opened its doors on April Fool's Day, 1928, on St. Anne's Street in a working-class Mid-City neighborhood. The current Mr. Bozo was born two months later, and the newly opened restaurant was his nursery. "In those days, nobody could afford a babysitter," Mr. Bozo said. "My parents put me under a table and they went to work." Soon after he could walk, he helped out as a delivery boy, then as a busboy and a waiter before graduating to the kitchen, where he has remained ever since.

Mr. Bozo the First came to America in the teens from his native Yugoslavia (the name "Bozo" is the old country equivalent of "Chris"). He disembarked in New York and then made his way to Louisiana to join the large population of fellow Yugoslavs who had found work harvesting oysters. So when Bozo opened his restaurant, he knew where to find the freshest, most supple oysters to serve his customers. The restaurant, located in Metairie since 1974, still prides itself on serving some of the finest oysters in town.

In New Orleans, one mixes up one's own oyster sauce — usually some mixture of horseradish, ketchup, and hot sauce. But Mr. Bozo the Second, who has been eating oysters his entire life, prefers a more delicate dressing. In a cocktail glass he mixes lemon juice, horseradish, pepper sauce, olive oil, and a dash of hot sauce "for color," and dips the oyster in the concoction with a fork. This, he explains, is the best way to taste the oyster's full flavor.

Mr. Bozo's father ran his restaurant on the philosophy that "if you have too many things on the menu, you start to do things wrong." So the menu remains simple today: oysters, crabs, shrimp, crawfish, but only one variety of fish — wild catfish from Bayou Des Allemandes, whose flesh Mr. Bozo believes is so superb that he doesn't care to serve an alternative. "It's not a pond-grown fish. It's a Mother Nature fish. You can't eat that fish with a fork," Mr. Bozo said. "You have to scoop it up with a spoon." The seafood is cooked in ancient blackened skillets — "Broiled, boiled, and stuffed," Mr. Bozo said. "But I'll grill it for fussy types."

Further specialties include the Shrimp Italian in a warm, lemony marinade, a lovely pale gumbo of chicken and andouille sausage, artichokes stuffed with a dense, savory tamping of seasoned breadcrumbs, and the usual roster of po' boy sandwiches. The menu offers standard seafood alternatives, such as fried chicken and hamburger steak, but no one in his or her senses would pass up a meal of the daily catch.

Broussard's

819 CONTI STREET

between Bourbon & Dauphine Streets

DAILY 5:30PM-10PM

☎ 504-581-3866

WHEN WILLIAM FAULKNER MOVED TO TOWN TO START HIS LITERARY CAREER, HE'D APPARENTLY GOTTEN THE MISTAKEN IMPRESSION THAT THE Volstead Act would make it hard to get a drink here, so he imported his own stash of bourbon, distilled on his family's Mississippi estate. To his relief, Faulkner discovered that alcohol was in ample supply in New Orleans, and he showed up regularly at saloons and speakeasies throughout the French Quarter. One of Faulkner's favorite haunts was Joseph Broussard's restaurant on Conti Street, not far from the writer's quarters in Pirate's Alley.

Broussard had a fondness for the city's artists and eccentrics; he was something of a character himself. Broussard had an unusual preoccupation with Napoleon Bonaparte, and when a customer ordered a glass of Courvoisier cognac (Napoleon's brand) Broussard would have a chorus of waiters belt out *La Marseillaise* while the customer wondered whether he'd ever get to sip his drink in peace.

Broussard was Cajun, not French, and his fondness for Napoleon stemmed more from a kinship of stature and temperament than nationality. He was a little man with an explosive temper, and he had exacting standards for his cooks—if a dish didn't pass muster, he'd snatch the plate and hurl it onto Conti Street.

Broussard apprenticed at Antoine's and once accompanied owner Jules Alciatore to France for culinary training. But Broussard wasn't content to go on laboring in someone else's kitchen. In 1920, he married a young Italian woman named Rosalie Borrello and opened Broussard's where it stands today, at 819 Conti Street, in what was once the stable and slave quarters of the Hermann-Grima estate (the main house is just over the high wall at the rear of the courtyard). The Creole a la carte menu bore an unsurprising resemblance to his former employer's — pompano en papillote, Brabant potatoes, fried softshell crab, marchand de vin — and Broussard hoped his restaurant would rise to equal footing with local fine-dining titans Galatoire's, Arnaud's and Antoine's. But it never acquired quite the same spruce, old-line savor. Antoine's remained the place New Orleans gentlemen took their families for a night out; Broussard's was where they took their mistresses.

Broussard died in 1966 (Rosalie passed away one month after him), and the restaurant was purchased by Italian owners, who renovated the dining rooms. In 1980, chef Gunter Preuss purchased Broussard's and ushered in a first-rate fusion menu. Appetizers include Delice ravigote Conti (bayou lump crabmeat in ravigote dressing, with a shrimp remoulade, gravlax, and crabmeat); casserole Florentine (baked crabmeat in an artichoke brie béchamel); mirliton Nicola (stuffed seafood with a tomato and roasted red pepper ragout). Entrees of note: redfish with crab-meat Herbsaint sauce; grilled pompano with pepper-crusted scallops; a saffron-flavored bouillabaisse; filet of beef brandon with boursin glaze; and sautéed veal slices layered with crabmeat.

In warm months, request a table in the courtyard, where a pair of sleek crape myrtles stand beside a failing wall of worn Louisiana brick.

CREOLE VS. CAJUN

The terms Creole and Cajun are often confusing to visitors to Louisiana, but French heritage aside, the two cultures have little in common. The city's Creoles were the offspring of French and Spanish settlers, and while their fortunes lasted, the Creoles were high-toned, caste-conscious cosmopolitans. Snobbish and hedonistic in equal measure, the Creoles began the New Orleanian traditions of good living and social politicking still cherished here today. The Creole aristocracy favored the culinary traditions of their ancestors and their homelands, but neither the French nor the Spanish customs could escape the others' influence. The French-trained cooks brought to the table a savory roux and a Parisian penchant for rich cream-based sauces. The Spanish, who were handed the deed to the city in 1762, introduced pepper to New Orleans cuisine and showed the French Creoles the many uses of the tomato, which they had long considered poisonous.

The Cajuns (Acadians), on the other hand, were peasant farmers from greater French Acadie—Maine, Nova Scotia, and New Brunswick—whom the British evicted from their homeland in the mid-1700s. The Acadians were of French ancestry themselves, and they trekked south to Louisiana where French was spoken. Unlike the Creoles, they shunned the city and settled in the fertile marshlands of south and southwestern Louisiana. Like their city cousins, Cajuns took their cuisine seriously, but a Cajun supper didn't have much in common with the refined banquetry of Creole society dinners. Cajuns went in for boisterous dances and feasts featuring spicy dishes such as jambalaya and piquante sauce cooked in neighborly quantities in a single pot.

Through the 1800s, the haute cuisine of the Creoles and the peasant traditions of Cajun cooking maintained a disdainful remove from one another. But in the 20th century, more open-minded chefs began fusing the two cuisines in a tasty confusion of culinary heritages.

Bruning's Seafood Restaurant

1924 WEST END PARKWAY

FRIDAY-SATURDAY 11AM-10:30PM

SUNDAY-THURSDAY 11AM-9:30PM

☎ 504-282-9395

NEW ORLEANS LIES IN A SAUCER OF LAND, AND IN THE SUMMER MONTHS, WHEN THE HUMIDITY SETTLES OVER THE CITY LIKE A PUDDLE OF SPILLED tea, the wisest thing to do is head for Lake Pontchartrain, which is the saucer's cooler rim. In the 1800s, people flocked here by the thousands, usually taking a mule-drawn streetcar from the city center. Heat-wearied citizens savored the mild breezes, cooled on the lake's temperate broads, and lunched on fresh seafood pulled daily from the lake's depths and sold up and down the shore.

Theodore Bruning came to New Orleans from Baden Baden, Germany, in the 1850s, when many German immigrants were fleeing political strife and the wake of crop famines in their native land. In 1859, Bruning opened a lakeside seafood house in West End Park, just across the New Basin Canal from the fishing village of Bucktown. He offered a menu of shrimp, crawfish, redfish, flounder, hard- and soft-shell crabs, served fresh and prepared simply — fried, boiled, or broiled.

In 1893, Captain John C. Bruning, Theodore's son, built a home for the family on the lakeshore, across the canal. John Bruning and his brother, Theodore, operated a pair of boathouses, renting skiffs to seafaring vacationers. When the weather turned rough, John Bruning would brave wind and lightning to pace the widow's walk with a pair of binoculars, looking out for crafts in distress. If he spotted someone in trouble, he and his brother would stage a rescue in their two-man rowboat. Over the years, John Bruning and his brother saved hundreds from drowning in the lake, which earned him a commendation from the Coast Guard.

Other than the restaurant and the skiff livery, the Brunings also turned a dollar in the lakefront's buzzing nightlife. In an adjacent pavilion, the family had slot machines and casino gambling. When jazz came of age, musicians such as Sweet Emma and Louis Armstrong played at the family's venue. Gigs at Bruning's were coveted. The pay wasn't any higher than in the French Quarter nightclubs, but performing musicians were welcome to all the soft-shell crabs they could eat, an enticement that kept the pavilion steadily booked.

In 1998, a storm destroyed the original restaurant, which relocated to a simple building just a few yards from the old structure. Bruning's still serves simple but superb seafood dishes: Gulf oysters, redfish, catfish, trout, tilapia, soft-shell crabs, flounder — all served fried or broiled at the customer's request. Bruning's is particularly fine at sunset, when a tide of scarlet light rises in the westward windows.

Bud Rip's

900 PIETY STREET AT BURGUNDY STREET

"WE DON'T HAVE ANY SET HOURS"

☎ 504-945-5762

A FEW OF THE REGULARS OF THE CLAPBOARD TAVERN AT THE CORNER OF PIETY AND BURGUNDY STREETS REMEMBER BUYING BEER HERE AS YOUNG CHILDREN with the management's full consent. Thirsty fathers, too tired after a long day working on the nearby riverfront to go fetch a beer themselves, would tell their kids to take a bucket to the bar's service window. The bartender kept an eye out for small palms smacking down handfuls of pennies on the windowsill — payment for a two-quart bucketful of beer.

The bar started pouring drinks in 1860 to the German, Irish, and Yugoslav workingmen who lived in the neighborhood. By the turn of the last century, the 9th Ward was one of the city's most dynamic districts. Nearby Saint Claude was Canal Street's working-class cousin, with dry goods shops, drug stores, banks, groceries, butcher shops, and haberdasheries lining the busy sidewalks. Schwegman's grocery store — a household name in New Orleans for most of the twentieth century — opened its first small shop on Piety Street opposite the bar.

Though it has changed hands and titles more times than anyone can remember, the room itself remains unchanged. The bar itself is unusually long, thirty-five feet or so, and it bespeaks a clientele who prefers hunching shoulder to shoulder within easy reach of the bartender to sitting at a table. At the far end of the bar, the old oyster counter extends at a right angle toward Burgundy Street. The bar no longer serves oysters, but the worn marble countertop still smells faintly of the Gulf.

The columns, walls, and wainscoting are sheathed, not with tin but pewter sheeting stamped with arabesques. The walls are painted brown, and the pewter is thick enough to silence the sound of outside traffic. On slow nights the room takes on a quality of silence that feels almost subterranean.

The backbar, which is made of mahogany and gently warping cherrywood veneer, arrived in 1911 courtesy of the woodshop at Dixie Brewing Company on Tulane Avenue. Before the Sherman Antitrust Act passed, breweries would commonly build backbars and even underwrite minor renovations for saloons that stocked their products exclusively. Only two early accoutrements are no longer in place here: the big glass sarsaparilla globe that used to sit on the bar (it is missed), and the urinal trough that ran below the footrail and emptied onto Piety Street (its absence is, gladly, tolerated).

A hundred years after the bar opened its doors, it was purchased by Bud Ripoll and the bar became known as Bud Rip's. The bar maintained its old gang of habitués — local politicians, Republicans mostly, and others who didn't care to let politics stand in the way of a cold drink. Ripoll made his most radical amendment to tradition in the early 1970s, when women were invited in.

Bud Rip's, with its atmosphere of weathered, downmarket grace, is one of New Orleans's greatest finds, though finding it will prove a challenge to newcomers to the Bywater. There is no sign out front, and in the evenings you have to ring a buzzer to get in the door — a security precaution in a neighborhood where barroom shootings were too common not long ago.

Vestibule, French Market, New Orleans.

Café du Monde

813 DECATUR STREET

across from Jackson Square

24 HOURS A DAY, 364 DAYS A YEAR

(CLOSED 6PM CHRISTMAS EVE-6PM CHRISTMAS DAY)

☎ 504-581-2914

I N THE LATE EIGHTEENTH CENTURY, WHEN ACADIAN PILGRIMS BEGAN MAKING THE TREK TO LOUISIANA FROM THEIR NATIVE NOVA SCOTIA, THERE WAS NO guarantee that provisions would last the length of the trip. Coffee, in particular, was difficult to come by, and the travelers took up the practice of stretching their supply with chopped and roasted endive root, or chicory. After the Acadians reached New Orleans, although coffee was plentiful, they preferred the bitter richness of the brew they'd grown used to on the trail, and persisted in the habit of adding chicory to their morning blend.

Café du Monde opened in 1860 as a modest coffee kiosk in the Halle des Boucheries in the French Market, selling its distinctive coffee to the Cajun farmers and fishermen who came to market their goods. The menu also included cold milk and French beignets—airy little pockets of fried dough, dusted with sloping drifts of powdered sugar—but nothing more.

Around the turn of the last century, the café moved into sturdier quarters, taking over the colonnaded patio at the end of the meat market, across from Jackson Square. In the 1920s, the café's proprietor wearied of doing business in what was then a rough part of town, and he sold the establishment to a wine merchant named Hubert Fernandez. The bill of sale included only four tables and a pair of chairs. Today, Fernandez's great-grandchildren run Café du Monde, which now seats 200 and has a second branch in neighboring Metairie.

THE OLD FRENCH MARKET

"*Once, if we may judge by the small model in the Cabildo, the old Halle des Boucheries of the French Market must have looked extraordinarily like a primitive Greek temple, on squat columns, all the space under the roof open to the air. Progress in the nineteenth century half enclosed the arcades with bathroom tiles, without thereby increasing the cleanliness, half screened them with wire, to accumulate more dirt, and painted the almost hidden pillars a dull oxblood red. A still more progressive twentieth century proposes to demolish it altogether and replace it by something not less sightly and a little more sanitary. This should not be hard. But the proposed change is resented by all who remember it in some happier, romantic stage before the war, when Choctaw women sold herbs and sassafras bark from grass-woven baskets and Negresses in tropically gay chignons dispensed hot drip coffee with a flavor of chicory... In the fish market...red snappers, rose-scaled, lie beside the slender silver-foil Spanish mackerel and pompano from the Gulf of Mexico. Lake trout from Pontchartrain are tied together by strips of palmetto... great round baskets of crabs go by, bedded in Spanish moss. Vast piles of shrimps, transparent shells from Barataria, are cooled under shovels of crushed ice. In their wire confines, the mahogany-red crawfish are in constant crawling motion; the monster swamp frogs squat under continual streams of water.*"

JOHN PEALE BISHOP, "NEW ORLEANS: DECATUR STREET"

FROM *The New Yorker*, JAN. 11, 1936

Café Sbisa

1011 DECATUR STREET

between St. Philip and Ursulines Streets

SUNDAY-THURSDAY 5:30PM-10:30PM

FRIDAY AND SATURDAY 5:30PM-11PM

SUNDAY JAZZ BRUNCH 10:30AM-3PM

☎ 504-522-5565

AT THE END OF THE NINETEENTH CENTURY, SAILORS WHO CAME TO PORT IN NEW ORLEANS DISTRUSTED BANKS AND BANKERS, PREFERRING INSTEAD TO leave their pay in the hands of a trusted tavernkeeper and to drink down the balance while their ships were at dock. At 1011 Decatur Street, just a few hundred feet from the Mississippi, Café Sbisa lay directly in the path of thirsty sailors, and the Sbisas, a family of Croatian immigrants, ran accounts for scores of seamen. Lower Decatur Street in the early 1900s was one of the less savory areas of the French Quarter—home to some of New Orleans's coarser brothels and open to all versions of vice. Mr. Sbisa made his money serving strong drinks, and also from the sporting women who operated in rooms on the café's second floor.

In the teens and twenties, Café Sbisa began attracting a better-heeled clientele, and it became a place where members of New Orleans's upper echelon came to gamble, or for a dalliance on the café's second floor. Politicians, actors, oil and cotton magnates all frequented the place, trusting the tight-lipped Sbisas to treat their doings here with due discretion. Mobster-cum-restaurateur "Diamond Jim" Moran was a fixture at the house poker games, which often ran until dawn.

In the 1970s, a local doctor bought the café and rehabilitated it into a first-rate Creole eatery. Today, the restaurant betrays little evidence of its shadowy past. The main dining room is broad and open, with a gleaming 1920s bar and red leather booths. The café's infamous second floor is now an open mezzanine, though the atmosphere is still intimate and drowsy.

The house specialty is the court-bouillon, a delicious Creole bouillabaisse of seasonal fish from the Gulf of Mexico, shrimp, crab claws, and scallops, though the menu offers other superb improvisations on local standards: blackened redfish topped with oysters and jumbo shrimp, crawfish beignets, Trout Eugene pan seared with crawfish tails and lump crabmeat, and Oysters Sbisa, oysters topped with spinach, bleu cheese, and apple-smoked bacon, served on the half shell.

BEIGNETS

Essentially a square doughnut with no hole, these fried pastries originated with the Acadian French who first settled south Louisiana. Served hot, and traditionally accompanied by café au lait, these delectable confections have been described in the *Los Angeles Times* as "an insidious Louisianian cousin of the doughnut that exists to get powdered sugar on your face." Beignet mix and dark roasted chicory blend coffee can be ordered from the Café du Monde mail order catalog (800) 772-2927 or online at www.cafe-dumonde.com

COFFEE ROASTERS

At the end of the nineteenth century, when communication with distant coffee producing countries was difficult, Magazine Street was lined with coffee importers who provided raw beans to hundreds of small coffee roasters throughout the United States. Many of the brands were christened with quintessential New Orleans names: Honeymoon, Tulane, St. Charles, French Opera, Dixieland, Loyola, and Monteleone. The American Coffee Company, founded in 1890, still operates at 800 Magazine Street, and continues to make its first product, French Market Coffee.

CASAMENTO'S RESTAURANT
OYSTERS
CASAMENTO'S
RESTAURANT
4330

Casamento's

4330 MAGAZINE STREET

SEPTEMBER 1-MAY 31: TUESDAY-SUNDAY

11:30AM-1:30PM, 5:30-9:30PM

CLOSED JUNE 1-SEPTEMBER 1

☎ 504-895-9761

"I N NEW ORLEANS THEY EAT OYSTERS ALL YEAR AROUND, BUT IN FAIRNESS TO THE OYSTERS, THEY SHOULDN'T—THEY ARE MUCH BETTER IN WINTER. THE Louisiana oyster in winter is still a solace to the man of moderate means, sold across the counter, opened, at sixty or seventy-five cents a dozen, and therefore usually eaten a couple of dozen at a time," wrote noted gourmand and journalist A. J. Liebling.

The Casamento family shares Liebling's reverence for a Gulf oyster in its prime. The off-season oyster is so distasteful to them that they close their restaurant on May 31st each year and reopen in September, when the bivalve spawning season is over, and the oyster is restored to full deliciousness.

Joe Casamento, an immigrant from Ustica, Italy, opened the restaurant in 1919 in the upper Garden District on Magazine Street. Casamento brought with him a Mediterranean fondness for ceramic tile, and had every surface covered with it, an order that took four tile companies to fill. The bright, echoing interior makes for an unusual restaurant-going experience, somewhat like dining in a locker room, but Joe Casamento wasn't the sort of restaurateur who fretted about ambience. A seafood restaurant, he thought, should be first and foremost a sanitary place, and indeed, outside of a surgical ward, you'd be hard pressed to find a more relentlessly germ-resistant room in town.

Beyond his devotion to cleanliness, Casamento was known as a shrewd and frugal businessman. One afternoon he was standing at the bar, shucking oysters for a clamoring lunch crowd. The door swung open and an oyster deliveryman stepped in. "Hate to tell you, but the prices just went up," he said. Casamento stopped shucking. He turned and went to the chalkboard behind him and adjusted the menu prices to reflect the cost hike, to the dismay of diners who'd already put their orders in. Other than oysters, which are sold raw or fried, and also served on sandwiches, the menu offers fried shrimp, trout, soft-shell crabs, and a very capable gumbo. Casamento's also makes an excellent oyster stew, a dish that is fairly hard to find in New Orleans.

KING CAKES

King Cakes, also known as Twelfth Night Cakes, are eaten in New Orleans between the Twelfth Night, January 6, and Ash Wednesday. The custom dates from twelfth-century France, where the cakes were baked to celebrate the feast of the three wise men who brought gifts to the infant Jesus. Originally containing a bean or pea, king cakes now contain a figurine of a baby. The person whose slice of cake contains the figurine traditionally provides the cake for next year's party. The cake is baked with cinnamon in the shape of a ring, is iced, and decorated with three colors of sugar: purple, symbolizing justice; yellow, symbolizing power; and green, symbolizing faith.

LOVE, SATCHMO

New Orleans native Louise Armstrong once said, "We all were brought up eating the same thing, so I will tell you: Red Beans and Rice with Ham Hocks is my birthmark." He was so fond of the dish that he used to sign his letters, "Red Beans and Ricely Yours."

ZATARAIN'S

In 1889, Emile Zatarain founded a company in New Orleans that still produces food products that reflect the distinctive flavors of the city's cuisine. For muffulettas, Zatarain's offers Italian Olive Salad Mix, Spiced Olives, and Fine Cut Chow Chow; for boiled seafood, a variety of shrimp and crab boils; for gumbos and jambalayas, seasonings such as cayenne pepper, Creole seasoning, étouffée base, and Gumbo Filé. 888-264-5460 or www.zatarains.com

Central Grocery

923 DECATUR STREET

between Dumaine and St. Philip Streets

MONDAY-SATURDAY 8AM-5:30PM

SUNDAY 9AM-5:30PM

☎ 504-523-1620

IN THE LATE 1800s, BLOOD FEUDS AMONG THE FRENCH QUARTER'S ITALIAN POPULATION AROSE WITH SUCH FREQUENCY THAT DECATUR STREET CAME TO be known by the ominous nickname "Vendetta Alley." At the center of the mayhem was an ongoing war between the Matranga and Provenzano crime families, who were both vying for control of the produce business on the Mississippi wharves. After the Provenzanos staged a bloody ambush against the Matrangas on May 1, 1890, David C. Hennessy, the city's chief of police, took a firm stand. "The Mafia cannot flourish," Hennessy said, "while I am chief of police." Less than six months later, on the night of October 15, Hennessy was found lying on Girod Street, riddled with shotgun wounds. "Dagoes," Hennessy reportedly gasped to a friend moments before he died.

Mayor Joseph A. Shakespeare issued the xenophobic order to arrest every Italian immigrant in the area. On scant evidence, police indicted nineteen Italian and Sicilian immigrants for varying degrees of involvement in the murder, ten of whom ultimately stood trial. A verdict was handed down on March 13, 1891, one which enraged the city's vengeance-hungry citizens. Seven of the men were acquitted and mistrials were declared for the remaining three. The next day, an armed mob swelled around the parish prison on Basin Street. Prison officials barred the door, but the angry crowd knocked it off its hinges with a battering ram. The vigilantes shot several prisoners as they huddled in their cells and executed others in the prison yard as they begged to be spared. Two men were thrust into nooses and hanged in the streets. Two months later, a Grand Jury held an investigation and declared the massacre justified.

But the anti-Italian bigotry that the murders so appallingly embodied did little to stop the migration of Italians coming to New Orleans in search of better lives. Salvatore Lupo, from Palermo, Sicily, arrived in New Orleans in the late 1890s. In 1906, he opened a small grocery on Decatur Street, in the heart of Vendetta Alley. Although life was tough for Italians here, Lupo's shop did well from the outset, receiving steady business from his countrymen, who were hungry for the foods they'd enjoyed in Italy: pastas, sausage, salami, prosciutto, Parmesan, olives, bread, and wine.

Farmers, fishermen, and dockworkers would come to Lupo's store to buy the makings for a traditional Italian lunch: salami, ham, cheese, olive salad, and round loaves of muffuletta bread. His customers lunched in the Italian style, eating each item separately. Without a proper table, it was an awkward undertaking. Patrons would perch on crates or barrelheads, trying to balance a confusion of paper trays on laps and cocked knees. Lupo made an unorthodox suggestion. What if he simply sliced the muffuletta loaf and made a sandwich of the whole spread? His customers liked the idea and the "muffuletta" became a house specialty.

A third generation of Lupos runs the grocery today. Salvatore Lupo's muffuletta sandwich is sold in restaurants across the city (and across the nation as well), but the Central Grocery is generally credited with the best muffulettas in town. The Lupos make their muffulettas with Genoa salami, Holland ham, Swiss cheese, olive salad, and, of course, soft muffuletta bread. Each morning they stack the back counter with a tall fortification of sandwiches wrapped in white butcher paper, and by early afternoon it's usually time to make more.

Simon Hubig Co.

2417 DAUPHINE STREET

between Mandeville and Spain Streets

NOT OPEN TO THE PUBLIC

☎ 504-945-2181

A CERTAIN STRIPE OF CUSTOMER OCCASIONALLY MAKES THE COMPLAINT THAT HUBIG'S FRIED TURNOVERS ARE NOT AS LARGE AS they used to be. Perhaps the customer's appetite has grown, or the pie looks smaller in grown-up hands; Hubig's Pies has been cutting its half-moon pies with the same cast-iron die for at least half a century, and probably a good while longer.

The Hubig's bakery on Dauphine Street is the only remaining evidence of what Simon Hubig, in the 1920s, hoped would one day become a coast-to-coast franchise. By 1929, Hubig, a German-born master baker based in Dallas, Texas, owned bakeries in Birmingham, Indianapolis, and New Orleans, with plans to carry the Hubig name even farther afield. But the stock market crash and the Depression cut the company's future short. After Hubig's death, all of his bakeries, save the New Orleans branch, were sold to outside interests. (Hubig's flagship bakery in Dallas was bought by Jack Ruby, who ran it as a nightclub in the years before his assassination of Lee Harvey Oswald.)

The Dauphine Street bakery and warehouse were purchased by Henry

Barret, who struggled to keep the company afloat in its first years as an independent outfit. Wartime sugar rationing might have killed the fledgling concern, had not the Hubig's employees surrendered their own sugar coupons to keep the bakery from shutting down.

Early on, the company sold a good number of "family pies," classic, circular desserts that made nightly appearances on dinner tables across southern Louisiana. But as women joined the workforce, and the American convention of sit-down, family dinners grew less common, Hubig's moved fewer of these family pies. Its fried and glazed fruit-filled turnovers, which could be eaten on the go, became the company's leading sellers.

Hubig's still operates out of its original, now wonderfully haggard, factory in the Bywater. Hubig's 8- and 9-inch family pies are still available at grocery stores and a handful of local restaurants. Hubig's turnovers, which come in a profusion of flavors—apple, lemon, peach, pineapple, chocolate, cherry, coconut, blueberry, banana, blackberry, and sweet potato—are sold at 3,500 or so small shops and groceries, though nowhere beyond a day's drive from New Orleans.

Commander's Palace

1403 WASHINGTON AVENUE

between Coliseum and Prytania Streets

MONDAY-FRIDAY 11:30AM-2PM, 6-10PM

SATURDAY 11:30AM-1PM, 6-10PM

SUNDAY 10:30AM-1:30PM

☎ 504-899-8221

ABUSINESSMAN MORE CAUTIOUS THAN EMILE COMMANDER MIGHT HAVE QUESTIONED THE WISDOM OF OPENING A RESTAURANT IN NEW ORLEANS during Reconstruction. The city was foundering in debt and corruption, and cholera and yellow fever ravaged the city, killing New Orleanians by the hundreds. Undaunted by the tumult, Commander opened his distinguished restaurant among the noble homes of the Garden District, at the corner of Washington Avenue and Coliseum Street, across the boulevard from Lafayette Cemetery I, where scores of yellow fever victims had been laid to rest.

The business was a success, and by 1900 Commander's Palace was attracting gourmets from around the globe. In the 1920's, under new management, the restaurant acquired a more licentious reputation. An indelicate class of riverboat captains made the place a regular haunt on their visits ashore, and while Commander's was no brothel, it was known as a place where gentlemen could come to pass an evening with "women who were not their wives." Mothers in the neighborhood instructed their daughters, when walking to school or the streetcar, to cross Washington Avenue and take the sidewalk bordering the cemetery rather than walk directly in front of the notorious restaurant.

In 1969, the Brennan family, New Orleans's fine dining dynasty, purchased the restaurant. Adelaide Brennan had the august Victorian mansion painted an unseemly teal blue, which ruffled feathers in this prim neighborhood. But the paint job has since become an accepted local irreverence — if you walk into a paint store in New Orleans and ask for a gallon of "Commander's blue," they'll produce a can and not bat an eyelid.

Under the Brennans' stewardship, the restaurant's haute Creole creations have garnered a long list of distinctions, and celebrated chefs Emeril Lagasse and Paul Prudhomme have both done stints in Commander's kitchen. The menu changes often, but specialties include Spicy Turtle Soup, Shrimp Tasso Henican with Five Pepper Jelly, Pecan Crusted Gulf Fish, Oysters in Champagne Gelee, Deep Dish Rabbit and Foie Gras Pie, Scuppernong Duck, Jack Daniel's Lacquered Mississippi Quail, and Chocolate Bread Pudding Soufflé.

The Court of Two Sisters

613 ROYAL STREET

between Toulouse and St. Peter Streets

DAILY 9AM-3PM, 5-10PM

☎ 504-522-7261

WHEN IT CAME TIME TO STOCK THEIR ARSENALS OF EVENING GOWNS FOR CARNIVAL SEASON, ARISTOCRATIC LADIES OF THE 1890S TURNED TO EMMA and Bertha Camors, a pair of cultured Creole sisters who ran a respected dressmaker's and "notions" shop at 613 Royal Street. In the 1800s, Creole aristocrats, Supreme Court justices, governors, and future United States President Zachary Taylor lived along this fashionable stretch of Royal Street. The illustrious address was a suitable one for the Camors sisters, who traced their lineage back to one of New Orleans's founding families. But in the early 1900s, Creole fortunes went into sharp decline, and many old families left the neighborhood. In 1906, with their clientele diminishing, Emma and Bertha abandoned the mansion at 613 Royal and moved into half of a shotgun house on North Dupre.

In the '20s and '30s the Royal Street mansion housed a series of short-lived businesses: a refreshment stand, a bistro and a speakeasy. In 1940, local entrepreneur Jimmy Cooper opened the Court of Two Sisters restaurant, which he ran until his death in 1956.

The Camors sisters died within two months of one another in 1944, and they left no survivors. In New Orleans, the swampy soil cannot accommodate conventional graves, and so the dead return to dust in above-ground "oven tombs" which require annual maintenance fees. When restaurateur Joe Fein took over the Court of Two Sisters in 1963, a city official mentioned to him that the rent on the Camors' crypt was overdue, and the departed sisters faced eviction. Fein agreed to shoulder the Camors'

[59]

Court of Two Sisters

debts, and the Fein family still sends fresh flowers to the ladies' grave each week.

The Court of Two Sisters hosts a daily jazz brunch and an all-you-care-to-eat buffet — an unexceptional assortment of traditional New Orleans dishes arrayed in the hulls of a pair of fiberglass johnboats. The main attraction is the rear courtyard, a spacious patio fogged in by a low green canopy of century-old wisteria, illuminated in the evenings by flickering gas lamps. The Court is best enjoyed in early spring, when the wisteria sags with lavender blossoms, and the scent of jasmine and sweet olive overwhelms the courtyard.

Leidenheimer Baking Co.

☎ 504-525-1575

I N THE LATE 1920s, NEW ORLEANS STREETCAR CONDUCTORS LAUNCHED A LONG AND VIOLENT STRIKE. BENNY AND CLOVIS MARTIN, THEM-selves a pair of former conductors who ran a French Quarter sandwich shop, sympathized with the workers and offered them free meals for the strike's duration. The Martin brothers served the men a simple sand-wich — roast beef drippings slopped over fried potatoes on French bread. When a striking conductor came into the Martins' shop, the brothers would call out, "Here comes another poor boy," and set a sandwich on the counter.

The strike eventually came to an end, but the strikers' fare endured, and before long "po' boys"—topped with a variety of fried Gulf seafoods (oysters, shrimp, softshell crabs, catfish), sausage, chicken, meatballs, or roast beef — were being sold in groceries, lunch joints, and taverns all over town. The first po' boys were made with traditional French bread, which was stoutest at the middle of the loaf and tapered on both ends. Po' boys made from the narrow ends of the loaf rather than its fat midsection tended to anger hungry customers who received them, so local bakeries began making long, symmetrical loaves, which yielded uncontroversial sand-wiches of uniform size.

The new bread—with its delicate crust and light, snowy interior—was something of a departure for the Leidenheimer Baking Company. In the days since George H. Leidenheimer started the bakery in 1886, he'd turned

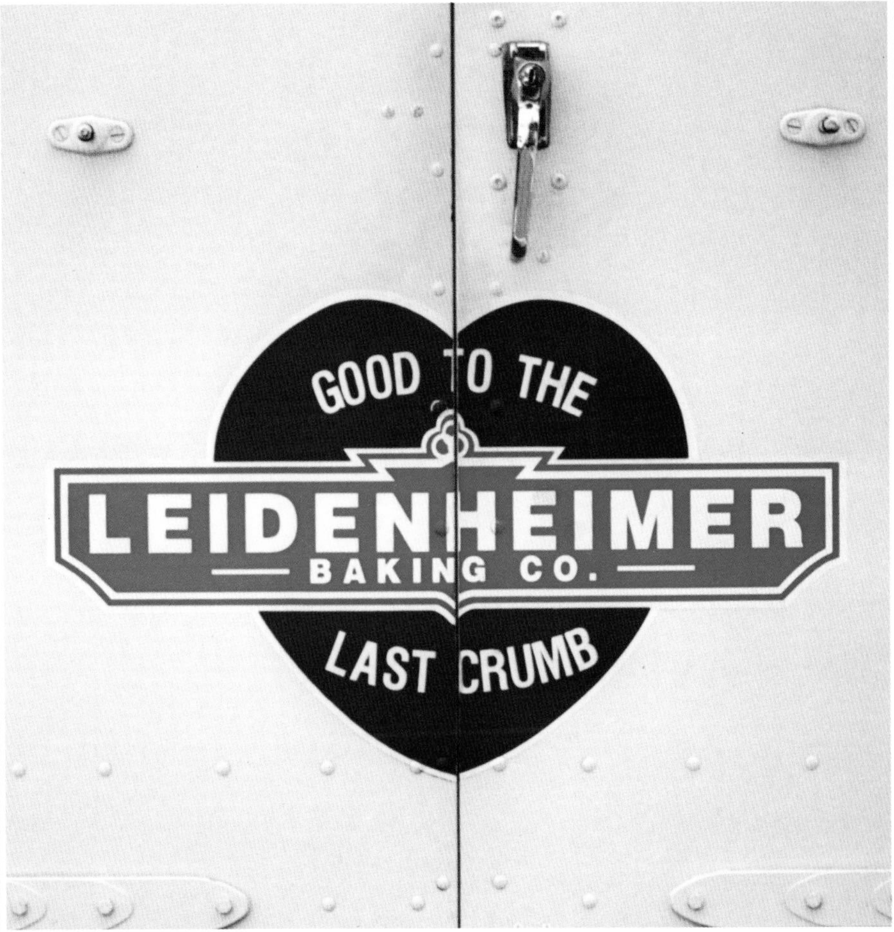
GOOD TO THE
LEIDENHEIMER
BAKING CO.
LAST CRUMB

out mostly the heavy sourdoughs and dense ryes and pumpernickels of his native Germany, delivering them throughout New Orleans with a fleet of mule-drawn wagons.

In 1905, Leidenheimer's moved from its first address on Dryades Street to a handsome brick building at 1501 Simon Bolivar Street. Leidenheimer asked the architects to work a couple of windows into the building's design—a rare caprice for a bakery, which does its work at night. The building's few windows wouldn't strike a non-baker as a noteworthy indulgence, but Leidenheimer was proud of them, and for a time, his bakery bore the slogan "The Daylight Bakery" (later discarded for "Good to the Last Crumb"). In its new, expanded quarters, Leidenheimer's could handily accommodate the city's appetite for the long, airy po' boy loaves, which drove the company's increasing success.

After Leidenheimer's death in 1918, the bakery passed to his son-in-law, Robert Whann. A fourth generation runs the bakery today. In the 1970s, the company closed its retail shop, but Leidenheimer breads—pistolettes, po' boy breads, muffulettas, and table breads—appear throughout New Orleans in grocery stores and restaurants.

LEIDENHEIMER JINGLE

Ooh la Leidenheimer,
That's what I said.
Ooh la Leidenheimer
That's French for bread.

Domilise's Po-Boy & Bar

5240 ANNUNCIATION STREET

at Bellecastle Street

MONDAY-SATURDAY 10AM-7PM

☎ 504-899-9126

OVER THE YEARS, SO MANY FEET HAVE LINGERED IN FRONT OF THE SAND-WICH COUNTER AT DOMILISE'S PO' BOY SHOP THAT A SHALLOW, UNEVEN hole has been worn into the linoleum — an accidental and oddly lovely exhibit of floorings past. The present, beige linoleum has been worn through to an older layer of orange tile. At the center of the stripe of wear is black concrete — a stratum of maximum impatience, where countless shoes have chafed and shuffled away those minutes that seem to lengthen when one's lunch order remains unfulfilled.

The shop opened around 1929 as an informal neighborhood bar in a room attached to Peter Domilise's house at Annunciation and Bellecastle Streets. It wasn't a grand establishment, just a place where neighborhood friends, mostly Domilise's countrymen from Sicily, could stop in for a drink. Domilise and his wife always had something to eat on hand — sandwiches, usually, which they gave away for free. They accepted money for drinks, but it seemed to the Domilises that there was something unneighborly in charging friends for a bite to eat. Ultimately, however, they saw that there might be a certain entrepreneurial wisdom in adding a limited menu, and so they built a sandwich bar on the Annunciation Street side of the room, selling po' boys exclusively.

After World War II, the business passed to the Domilises' son, Sam. Sam Domilise was a civic leader in this working-class Uptown neighborhood, and after hours, the shop became a sort of unofficial municipal meeting room, where members of the community would gather to puzzle out pressing issues in the 13th

Ward. Meetings were often interrupted by late-night phone calls from Domilise's constituents, who explained in slurred, apologetic tones that, well, they were in a bit of a fix and needed help posting bail. Domilise usually complied.

Sam Domilise died in 1981, and now the shop is run by Dot Domilise — "Miss Dot" to anybody who's been here more than once. It remains a humble room, with walls of wood paneling and a drop ceiling. Behind the beverage bar is an informal beer can museum, which showcases yellowing tin cans of Jax, Dixie, and Falstaff.

Domilise's still serves only po' boys on untoasted loaves of Leidenheimer bread. The house specialty is the roast beef po' boy. It comes with both yellow and Creole mustard. Order it with the messy ladling of brown gravy, and when you're finished, be grateful for the hand-washing sink at the far end of the room.

Emeril's Delmonico

1300 ST. CHARLES AVENUE

at Erato Street

MONDAY-FRIDAY 11:30AM-2PM

SUNDAY-THURSDAY 6PM-10PM

FRIDAY-SATURDAY 6PM-11PM

SUNDAY 10:30AM-2PM

☎ 504-525-4937

S LATE AS THE 1880s, BOXING WAS STILL CONSIDERED A BRUTAL, VULGAR AMUSEMENT UNFIT FOR CIVILIZED AMERICANS, AND THE SPORT REMAINED illegal in all fifty states. Yet a fervor for boxing was rapidly taking hold among America's middle and upper classes. The sport found particular approval in New Orleans, where vice and bourgeois virtues had always managed an easy coexistence. In 1890 the Crescent City became the first in the nation to legalize prizefights.

The early matches were not genteel affairs. The rules were loose, the refereeing lax, and the matches often ending with a fighter lying dead or paralyzed. Three years after the boxing ban was lifted, pugilists Andy Bowen and Jack Burke fought a gruesome seven-hour-and-nineteen-minute stalemate in New Orleans, a fight that still holds the record for the sport's longest bout. Sadly, Bowen, a local favorite, was killed in the ring a year later, to the considerable horror of New Orleans's newfound boxing fans.

But the city's enthusiasm for boxing endured, and by the turn of the century it was a favored recreation at local gymnasiums and gentlemen's athletic clubs. In 1911, when Anthony LaFranca purchased Delmonico, a venerable eatery at St. Charles Avenue and Erato Street, he had a second story added to the building and installed an informal gym there. When conversation in the restaurant lulled, the sound of boxing gloves thudding overhead resounded in the dining room.

LaFranca had immigrated to New Orleans from Sicily in 1903 and found work at Tranchina's Restaurant on Lake Ponchartrain, where he began a romance with the owner's granddaughter, Marie Masset. When LaFranca and Masset were wed in 1916, his new wife asked that he give up the upstairs boxing studio along with his bachelorhood. The gym was converted to an apartment for the LaFranca family.

In 1997, chef Emeril Lagasse purchased Delmonico from LaFranca and Masset's daughters and devised a new menu featuring contemporary Creole dishes — barbecued shrimp with garlic bread, shrimp remoulade with fried eggplant, crab salad with herb-caper dressing, pan fried redfish meunière, broiled beef tenderloin with Creole seasoning, and jumbo shrimp stuffed with crabmeat, a cherished holdover from the former menu.

Under Lagasse's stewardship, Delmonico underwent a costly and thorough redesign. Though its quietly sumptuous dining rooms are a far cry from the plaid wallpaper and crimson tablecloths of the LaFranca days, the feeling of the old restaurant survives in subtle details: the rustic wooden carts stacked with silverware and water pitchers, the worn leather upholstery in the lounge, the wood-framed photographs of Anthony LaFranca posing with local pugilists, which still adorn the restaurant's walls.

Ernst Café

600 SOUTH PETERS STREET

at Lafayette Street

DAILY 11AM-6PM

☎ 504-525-8544

I N 1902, IN A TWO-STORY BRICK BUILDING ON THE CORNER OF SOUTH PETERS AND LAFAYETTE STREETS, JOSEPH AND MALCOLM ERNST OPENED A SMALL CAFÉ catering to the warehouse hands who made their livings in the neighborhood. The café flourished during Prohibition, when the brothers converted a back room into a popular speakeasy. A later owner (who, in keeping with local propriety, shall remain unidentified), acquired the building in the 1940s, and divided the second floor into cramped berths known as "cribs" where prostitutes plied their trade.

The decor downstairs has changed little over the café's century in business. The eggnog-colored tin walls, embossed with fleurs-de-lis, are in surprisingly good shape, as is the antique mahogany backbar. Midroom, a staircase ascends conspicuously toward an unseen upper reach. Upstairs, however, the cribs have been demolished, and the room is now a comfortable, airy space with avocado bead-board wainscoting, and a wall of French doors that open onto a pleasant balcony.

The striking element of the café's decor is the barroom floor, which is inlaid with a mosaic pattern of inverted swastikas. The owners are quick to explain that the floor was installed at least a hundred years before Hitler's rise to power. A plaque defends the design as "a symbol for peace, which appeared on the Great Wall of China, and at the pyramids."

The café still serves casual, inexpensive bar food — burgers, fries, buffalo wings, pecan fried catfish — to a clientele of regulars, and also does a heavy evening business at the bar.

CENTRAL BUSINESS DISTRICT

When his father died in 1800, Bernard de Marigny became the wealthiest fifteen-year-old in America, and probably the most prosperous man in New Orleans. But by the time he was twenty-three, Marigny's gambling habits had driven him to the brink of ruin. In a desperate effort to restore his fortune, Marigny subdivided and sold off portions of his estate, a swath of land below the French Quarter, and thus the Faubourg (the French term for suburb) Marigny became the newest district in the growing city.

Marigny named the streets himself. The street where Creole gentlemen kept their quadroon mistresses, he pointedly titled "Love Street." One he called Champs Elysees, or Elysian Fields, after the Parisian boulevard. Another he titled Rue de Craps, after the game that ultimately destroyed him.

By 1828, Marigny's luck on the craps table had not improved, and his debts threatened to consume what few assets he had left. An American businessman named Samuel J. Peters then made Marigny an offer. He wanted to buy the Creole's faubourg, raze it, and on its ashes build a new commercial and cultural citadel, with opulent hotels, banks, new shipping docks, theaters, and cotton gins. But when they met to finalize the deal, Marigny's wife and co-signatory was nowhere to be found. Peters, already weary of dealing with the slippery Marigny, suspected he was being conned and left in a fury.

Peters carried his vision across the commons, to the marshy Faubourg

St. Marie, and began construction on what would in time become the Central Business District. In a riot of industry, Peters and his American colleagues filled in the swamp and built grand hotels, bustling wharves, and commodity brokerages. They walled the streets with Yankee-style brick-front row buildings, blatantly disdaining the French and Spanish architecture of the city's Creole wards. A street running parallel to the riverfront was named Peters Street in the entrepreneur's honor, and the name remains today. Most of Bernard de Marigny's fanciful street names have since been discarded.

Galatoire's

209 BOURBON STREET

between Iberville and Bienville Streets

TUESDAY-SATURDAY 11:30AM-9PM

SUNDAY 12PM-9PM

☎ 504-525-2021

"I'M TAKING BLANCHE TO GALATOIRE'S," STELLA KOWALSKI TELLS STANLEY IN TENNESSEE WILLIAMS'S *A STREETCAR NAMED DESIRE*. "WHAT ABOUT MY SUPPER?" Stanley says. "I'm not going to no Galatoire's for supper." No, indeed, but it must have amused Williams to imagine his coarse invention trampling the atmosphere in this genteel bistro.

Galatoire's was, in fact, the playwright's favorite local restaurant, and though he generally dined at his preferred table (beside the plate glass window on the Bourbon Street side of the room), he, like everyone else, was not allowed to reserve a spot ahead of time.

Jean Galatoire, a French immigrant from the foothills of the Pyrenees, instituted the no-reservations policy when the restaurant opened in 1905, a decision which has led to a century of consternation for New Orleans's tourists and locals who clamor daily for tables here. Charles De Gaulle, on a visit to New Orleans, was outraged when the proprietors would make no exception for him, and he dined elsewhere. Others have handled the policy more obligingly: U.S. Senator J. Bennett Johnston was standing in line when a call from President Reagan came for him on Galatoire's house phone. The senator stepped inside to take the call and afterwards headed back to join his party on the sidewalk. On Fridays before Christmas, when an appearance at Galatoire's is a Yuletide rite among old-line New Orleanians, patrons customarily hire surrogates to hold their place in line, which usually snakes far down Bourbon Street.

The policy underwent mild amendment in 1999, when the owners renovated and reopened the upstairs dining rooms (closed during World War II, because of the shortage of men to wait on tables) and began accepting reservations; the main dining room downstairs, true to tradition, remains first come, first served.

Most days, Fridays in particular, local politicians, lawyers, and well-heeled retirees arrive for a late-morning lunch and spend the afternoon in a leisurely choreography of table hopping, visiting with friends and associates, catching up on the latest doings in town, and usually downing the restaurant's famed martinis in high volume. ("Come for lunch, stay for dinner, go home in a wheelbarrow," is the restaurant's unofficial credo.)

The main dining room, insulated from the tumult of Bourbon Street only by its plate glass windows, exudes an unaffected grace. A thicket of two-bladed fans hangs from the ceiling; the fleurs-de-lis stenciled in fading gold paint on the kelly green walls and the old tile floors belie any suggestion of recent renovation.

The menu, too, remains elegant and old-fashioned: oysters en brochette, oysters Rockefeller, crabmeat maison, fried eggplant, Brabant potatoes, shrimp remoulade, grilled pompano in meunière sauce, Galatoire Grand Goute, trout meunière amandine, lamb chops béarnaise. You can get almost any dish topped with lump crabmeat Yvonne — an appetizing addition to everything except the bread pudding.

Jean Lafitte's Old Absinthe House

240 BOURBON STREET

between Iberville and Bienville Streets

SUNDAY-THURSDAY 9:30AM-2AM

FRIDAY-SATURDAY 9:30AM-4AM

☎ 504-523-3181

IN EDGAR DEGAS'S 1876 PAINTING *L'ABSINTHE*, A WOMAN SITS SLUMPED MID-MORNING BEFORE AN OPALESCENT GLASS OF ABSINTHE, HER FEATURES LEADEN with despair. It was surely a feeling Degas knew first-hand; among his other alcoholic appetites, the painter was a heavy absinthe drinker himself.

Three years before Degas made this bleak work, he had journeyed to New Orleans to stay for a time with his French Creole relatives in their home on Esplanade Avenue. He devoted his days to his easel and created the famous painting *A Cotton Office in New Orleans* here, along with a number of lesser-known portraits. It isn't certain where Degas did his drinking after wrapping up a day's work, but a thirst for the vivid chartreuse liquor he'd developed a taste for in France would have surely carried him to the Absinthe Room, a casual tavern at 240 Bourbon Street.

Despite its nasty side effects—delirium tremens, kidney failure, hallucinatory fugues, cirrhosis, and death—absinthe was hugely fashionable among Victorian Orleanians and found its aficionados among the musicians, pimps, and madams of Storyville, the poets and artists of the French Quarter, and the spreeing out-of-towners eager to try an exotic new stupor. The Absinthe Room was the epicenter of the absinthe fad, and its infamous cocktail attracted famous patrons. Oscar Wilde, Mark Twain, Robert E. Lee, Sarah Bernhardt, Walt Whitman, and William Makepeace Thackeray all stopped in for a taste.

The Absinthe Room first hung out its sign in 1874, when mixologist Cayetano

Ferrer created the absinthe frappe, a mind-numbing mixture of absinthe and anisette poured over ice. Sixty years earlier, local lore has it that Andrew Jackson met with pirates Pierre and Jean Lafitte in the rooms above the bar (then a corner grocery) to plan the city's defense against the advancing British fleet. There isn't much to support the claim, but the rumor gave owner Tony Moran sufficient grounds to add the pirate's famous name to the sign.

During Prohibition the Old Absinthe House continued operating as a speakeasy. Local authorities had plans to raid the tavern and to smash its antique marble bar. News of the raid was leaked, however, and the bar was smuggled out. The bar never returned to the Old Absinthe House. It did, however, appear years later at a now-defunct Bourbon Street saloon called "The Absinthe House Bar," an unsubtle advertisement for the historic marble slab.

The Old Absinthe House has held onto a few of its original furnishings, including the old water dripper, a beautiful miniature hydrant of dark emerald marble. An old chandelier, hazy with dust, hangs above the dented copper bar. But the old fittings seem out of place with recent additions to the bar's decor: a dense confetti of business cards stapled to every wall, and a hanging garden of football helmets and sports paraphernalia that dangles over the bartenders' corral.

In 1912, absinthe was banned in the United States, but bartenders at Old Absinthe House make a reasonable facsimile of the traditional cocktail using the locally manufactured spirit Herbsaint, whose label features an etching of the bar itself. To their credit, they make a point of going through the whole painstaking process: placing a sugar cube on a perforated absinthe trowel over a tumbler and patiently dousing the cube with a stream of green liquor until it dissolves into the glass.

OLD ABSINTHE HOUSE FRAPPÉ

Fill a thin glass with finely crushed ice. Add a half-teaspoonful of simple syrup. Add 1 oz. Herbsaint. Stir, using a long-handled spoon, with an up-and-down motion until outside of glass is frosted. Strain into another glass that has been chilled. Remove ice from original glass, pour drink back into it and serve.

ABSINTHE: A HISTORY

Potent herbal liqueur associated in the nineteenth century with legends of artistic decadence, insanity, and suicide. Vincent van Gogh, Paul Gauguin, Charles Baudelaire, Paul Verlaine, and Oscar Wilde were among those who partook of absinthe for its purported ability to enhance creativity. In France, where it was most popular, absinthe was commonly called La Fée Verte, or Green Fairy, because of its emerald color, which became cloudy and opalescent when water was poured into it through a cube of sugar that had been placed on a slotted absinthe spoon, or trowel. It became a popular drink in New Orleans as well, in part because of the French character of the city. In 1912, absinthe was outlawed in the United States because of its allegedly narcotic qualities. A version of absinthe, without the supposedly toxic ingredient, wormwood, is now made in New Orleans under the name of Herbsaint.

VINTAGE ADVERTISEMENT FOR LEGENDRE HERBSAINT

CIRCA 1930s

"French in name, French in origin, and French in its sophisticated exotic appeal, Legendre Herbsaint is a drink distinctly European in character. Its very appearance differs from all other drinks. In its original state Herbsaint is a transparent greenish amber. Mixed with water or ice as in a frappe, Herbsaint becomes an opaque beverage whose gyrating whorls of coalescent strata have a distinct opalescent hue.

"This refreshing and stimulating beverage pleases the palate of the connoisseur and man about town alike, and is reminiscent of the charm and unique appeal of New Orleans, in whose Vieux Carré (French Quarter) it has attained its greatest popularity. To drink Herbsaint is to recall the glories of the past, to renew acquaintance with the romance and glamour of bygone days."

Lafitte's Blacksmith Shop

941 BOURBON STREET

between St. Phillip and Dumaine Streets

DAILY 11AM-2AM OR LATER

☎ 504-593-9761

LAFITTE'S BLACKSMITH SHOP, THE COLLAPSING FRENCH PROVINCIAL COTTAGE AT BOURBON AND ST. PHILLIP STREETS, PROFESSES TO BE THE OLDEST STRUCture in America housing a tavern, and by all appearances, it's a reasonable claim. The wooden shutters have aged to an antlerish sheen; broad plaques of plaster are missing from the walls, revealing bricks worn to the sandy, underlying layer; the roof gently swells and rolls like the surface of a mild sea, and the dormer windows list like buoys on the tide. Inside, the place feels like a pleasant dungeon. The red cypress rafters are indelibly shadowed with centuries of tobacco smoke, like the great chimney in the center of the room. There are almost no electric lights here; instead, candles shine a muted glimmer on the chimney's veneer of aging creosote. At the end of the dented copper bar, there is a smog-dimmed portrait of Jean Lafitte, a man who accumulated more epithets than any other figure in New Orleans lore: the Bourbon Street Blacksmith, the Slave Trader, the French Corsair, the King of Smugglers, the Gentleman Rover, the Hellish Bandit, the Soldier of Jackson, and many others.

After the turn of the nineteenth century, shortly before Louisiana joined the United States, brothers Pierre and Jean Lafitte began making a name for themselves on the coast, plundering ships in the Gulf and selling their ill-gotten wares to American and Creole merchants. In 1809, they came to New Orleans and opened a blacksmith shop at Bourbon and St. Peter Streets. The shop was known less for its smithy than for the other goods it carried. Slaves could be purchased here, along with

every variety of pirated freight, at prices well below the legitimate market rate. Lafitte ran a lucrative, far-reaching business (he liked to boast that he had made half of New Orleans's merchants rich), and generally went unmolested by the law. Governor William Claiborne did once post a batch of handbills around New Orleans, offering $500 for Lafitte's capture. Lafitte promptly plastered the city with a more tempting counteroffer: $5,000 for the governor's head.

In the autumn of 1814, a fleet of British ships appeared off Louisiana's coast. Its intentions were clear: to claim the lands of the Louisiana Purchase and halt America's westward expansion at the Mississippi River. British Lt. Col. Edward Nicholls dispatched a messenger to Jean Lafitte, offering him a large sum of money and captainship of a British frigate if the pirate would join their side. Lafitte asked for fifteen days to consider the proposal. Knowing that his band, made up mostly of Americans, would mutiny if he went to the British side, Lafitte sent a letter to Governor Claiborne offering his services in the impending battle, declaring with diplomatic sincerity, "I am the stray sheep, wishing to return to the sheepfold." The Americans responded to this offer by raiding Lafitte's redoubt on Grand Terre Island, though the privateer himself escaped.

With a British attack looming, anxieties mounted for Governor Claiborne and Andrew Jackson, who knew the two-ship navy stationed here would make a feeble showing against British assault. There might be something, the now fearful Americans reasoned, in Lafitte's offer after all. Lafitte, surprisingly, bore Claiborne and Jackson no ill will over the recent raid and joined the American cause.

On January 8, 1815, under a dense white fog, the British made the assault on Jackson's line. But Jackson's soldiers, aided by Lafitte's men and materiel, made their stand, and the battle was a gory rout. At the end of the day, more than two thousand men had fallen on the British side; on Jackson's, merely six. Soon afterward, the future president drafted a letter extending to Lafitte his "private friendship and high esteem" for the pirate's role in the Battle of New Orleans.

Whether Lafitte himself did business in the half-timber, half-brick house at 941 Bourbon Street is a matter of some debate. But it's certain that over its long life, the house has seen more use as a saloon than as a blacksmith shop. The first tavern reportedly opened here in 1772, followed by many others over the last two-and-a-quarter centuries. Lafitte's changed hands most recently in the early 1950s, supposedly after owner Tom Caplinger drove the business into debt by extending a fortune in free drinks to friends such as Tennessee Williams and Lucius Beebe.

Mandich Restaurant and Bar

IN THE TEENS AND TWENTIES, WHEN CASINOS THRIVED ACROSS THE INNER HARBOR NAVIGATIONAL CANAL, IN THE SUBURB OF ARABI, MANDICH SHARED IN the success. Dealers would stop by late at night for a plate of home-cooked food, and gamblers, who had perhaps reached the bottoms of their pockets, were grateful to have somewhere to go for a decent, inexpensive bite to eat. Locals came here, too. In the days before television began to keep people home in the evenings, Mandich was one of the 9th Ward's public living rooms, the first place people went at the end of the workday. They'd spend hours here, chatting with neighbors, heading home only when the evening had grown old and it was time to go to bed.

John Mandich opened the restaurant in 1922 in a frame building formerly used as a pool hall. Mandich started with a bare-bones menu, selling mostly sandwiches and seafood. In those early days, the restaurant was a one-man operation, but Mandich was such an eager entrepreneur that when someone called him with a delivery order, he'd hop on the bicycle that he kept in the kitchen, hang a sign on the door, and hope he didn't miss much business during his absence.

Mandich stood behind the bar here for twenty-five years, and in 1947 he sold the business to partners Lloyd English and Anthony Matulich (nephew of Chris Matulich, the Chris behind Ruth's Chris Steak House), who later sold his share. Soon after the new owners took over, the neighborhood began to decline. In 1949, the local streetcar lines — St. Claude and Desire — were uprooted to accommodate bus routes, which city officials claimed would be faster and more efficient, though the removal of the streetcars only helped spur the general deterioration already taking place here. And in the 1960s, when the pattern of white flight worsened, the neighborhood grew destitute, and most of the shops, bakeries, and restaurants that had for years thrived along St. Claude Avenue moved on as well. But Mandich remained, and English and his family worked earnestly to keep the restaurant going. They expanded the menu to include more plate dinners and hot lunches, and kept their doors open morning-'til-morning, from 7:30am to 12:30am. English and Matulich closed the restaurant a single day each week: Tuesdays, because law forbade the sale of alcohol on election days, and the owners couldn't bear the thought of missing two days of sales even one or two weeks a year.

After the death of Lloyd English Sr., Lloyd Jr. took over the restaurant. English decided he'd rather shorten Mandich's hours than leave the restaurant open without being around to oversee it. Now Mandich serves lunch Tuesday through Saturday, and dinner on Friday and Saturday nights only. Best bets are the turtle soup, crisp trout Mandich, garlic stuffed pork loin, roasted duck in sweet potato sauce, oysters Bordelaise and Rockefeller, ham and red bean soup, trout topped with hollandaise and crabmeat, and oysters in a savory garlic oil.

MAGNOLIA
BRAND
BARATARIA
SHRIMP
·FRESH·FROM·THE·GULF·
WASH OFF W

Mandina's

3800 CANAL STREET

at Cortez Street

MONDAY-THURSDAY 11AM-10:30PM

FRIDAY-SATURDAY 11AM-11PM

SUNDAY 12PM-9PM

☎ 504-482-9179

MANDINA'S RESTAURANT DOESN'T SEEM ALL THAT INTERESTED ONE WAY OR ANOTHER ABOUT THE FACT THAT IT'S GETTING OLD, BUT THE GRAVITY OF its years shows in the dining room, where everything is gently settling out of skew. The old photographs on the wall have not hung level for some time. A liquor bottle on a sagging shelf leans forward in its perch with the faintly fearful stance of a man looking over a cliff. The drawers beneath the rear counter, when the bartender pulls them out past the tipping point, tilt suddenly floorward with a quiet thud. The dining room is bright and overlit, and there are no table linens here, just flecked Formica, which reflects the red and yellow glow of the neon signs out front. Sure, the restaurant could go in for the sorts of Old World affectations you find down in the French Quarter, but why bother? The same families have been coming here for generations and they like Mandina's as it is.

Until the 1920s, Sebastian Mandina ran a small grocery in Mid-City at the intersection of Canal and Cortez Streets. Prohibition presented Mandina with a lucrative sideline: making bathtub hooch and selling it from under the counter of his shop. He wasn't the only one with the idea, and it wasn't long before a competitor ratted him out to the authorities. The enterprising grocer was in and out of jail, and his sons, Anthony and Frank, thought it might be easier to abandon the bootlegging business and turn Mandina's into a respectable neighborhood restaurant, which they ultimately did after Prohibition, in 1932.

The restaurant served Creole and Italian dishes, priced reasonably so that working-class people could afford to dine here more than once a week. Along with its roster of regular dishes, the restaurant offered a cyclical menu of daily specials: beef stew on Tuesdays, stuffed bell peppers on Wednesdays, Italian specials on Thursdays, fish on Fridays for Catholic diners, beef on Saturdays, turkey on Sundays, red beans and rice on Monday night. Tommy Mandina, who runs the restaurant today, sticks to the weekly rotation faithfully. "We're not one of those joints where people go to eat what the chef created," Mandina said. "Who cares what the chef created? People here want to eat what they're used to eating."

In addition to its weekly specials, the restaurant is also known for its turtle soup — made with veal here — which the Mandinas regularly ship to customers who have moved away and are homesick for the rich stew.

Mandina's bar is also a cherished neighborhood institution. The far end is known to Mandina's regulars as "the corner" and for decades, gangs of politicians, businessmen, and gossip connoisseurs have gathered there to drink strong cocktails and discourse on the day's events.

MONDAY TRADITION: RED BEANS AND RICE

The Mandinas place a high value on tradition and disdain restaurants that serve red beans every day of the week. In the days before automatic washing machines, New Orleanians customarily cleaned their linens on Monday. The chore took all day, so people made red beans and rice, which could simmer for hours untended.

Morning Call Café

3325 SEVERN AVENUE

between North Hullen and 17th Streets

OPEN DAILY, 24 HOURS A DAY

☎ 504-885-4068

WHEN TOURISTS VISIT THE FRENCH QUARTER IN THE MOOD FOR BEIGNETS AND COFFEE, MOST STOP IN AT CAFÉ DU MONDE. BUT FOR MORE THAN A century, locals preferred the Morning Call Café, a coffee stand on the narrow wedge of land where Decatur Street veers off toward Esplanade Avenue. The Morning Call attracted a diverse clientele, and owners still recall a few of the esoteric regulars who hung around the café's French Quarter address. "Suitcase Tony" who, on a trip to Miami, survived seven gunshot wounds to his head, and could pour milk into his ear and let it trickle from his nose, to the amazement and distress of his fellow patrons. For years, a man known as "Wolfman" worked the graveyard shift as a beignet roller. He'd let out a howl each night at midnight and often worked his shift in costume—sometimes in a gladiator's helmet, sometimes in an Elvis Presley jumpsuit—though the Morning Call logo tattooed on his arm was a permanent part of his ensemble. One of the old waiters here gravely swore that he'd seen Lucifer trot into the café one night on a pair of cloven hoofs.

Joseph Jurasich, an immigrant from Austria-Hungary, opened the café in 1870, serving chicory coffee and beignets. With the onset of the automobile age, the Morning Call's stock in trade turned to curbside service, but in the early 1970s, when Decatur Street underwent a revitalization project at the expense of free parking spots, the owners held a jazz funeral for the old café, and relocated the business to a low-lying Metairie shopping center at Severn Avenue and 17th Street. The new address doesn't offer much in the way of antique charm, but once you cross the threshold, the Morning Call's appeal hardly seems diminished by the relocation. They've brought along the original sign — a beautiful, light-bulb-studded mahogany arch — as well as the old stools and weathered marble countertops, which are yellow with age and a century's worth of spilled café au lait. The ink-black chicory coffee, rich and bitter, is strained through hand stitched fabric filters and poured from old kettles. The beignets here are still hand rolled and cut on a flour-dusted table, then fried in small batches, and are incomparably tasty and light.

> *"We were rarely home at dinner, but our breakfasts and occasional dinners were more luxurious than if we had provided for ourselves. Excellent coffee, French bread, radishes, and strawberries at breakfast; and at dinner, broth, fowls, beefsteak, with peas, young asparagus, salad, new potatoes, and spinach, all well cooked; claret at dinner, and coffee worthy of Paris after it; this was the kind of provision with which we were favoured."*
>
> HARRIET MARTINEAU, *"The Haunted House"*
> FROM *Retrospect of Western Travel*, 1838

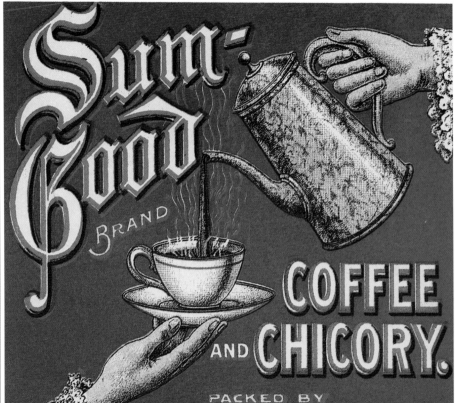

Napoleon House Bar and Café

500 CHARTRES STREET

at St. Louis Street

MONDAY-THURSDAY 11AM-12AM

FRIDAY-SATURDAY 11AM-1AM

SUNDAY 11AM-7PM

☎ 504-524-9752

IN THE EARLY 1900s, GIUSEPPE IMPASTATO, A SICILIAN IMMIGRANT, OPENED A SMALL MARKET AT 500 CHARTRES. HE CALLED IT THE NAPOLEON HOUSE grocery, in tribute to Nicholas Girod's failed plot. The grocery flourished, selling drinks and 10-cent sandwiches to workers from the nearby Mississippi docks, and in 1920, Impastato bought Napoleon's would-be refuge for $10,000. During Prohibition, the grocery sold whiskey from a backroom cask, and after Repeal, Impastato converted the front room to a full-service saloon. An opera lover, Impastato insisted that only opera and classical music be played on the house phonograph, a convention upheld by Sal Impastato, who is Giuseppe's grand-nephew and the Napoleon House's current proprietor.

The bar is still a placid getaway from the clamor of the upper French Quarter, serving food and drinks in an atmosphere of elegant decay. The stucco walls show only ragged snatches of fading gold paint, but sentimental patrons refuse to let the owners put on a fresh coat. The hanging lamps cast a feeble yellow light and lend the place a comfortable gloom. Large French windows open on to St. Louis Street, and the room often echoes with the clatter of a passing horse-and-carriage tour. Today, the Napoleon House is best known for its Pimm's Cup cocktails, and for its muffuletta, which, in violation of local tradition, is served hot.

Nick's Bar

2400 TULANE AVENUE

at South Conti Street

MONDAY-FRIDAY 3PM-CLOSING

SATURDAY 5PM-CLOSING

SUNDAY 6PM-CLOSING

☎ 504-821-9128

ONE AFTERNOON IN 1918, NICK CASTROGIOVANNI PAID A VISIT TO HIS BROTHER, WHO OWNED A FAILING SALOON IN A SMALL FRAME HOUSE ON the corner of Tulane and South Conti Streets. His brother was in a despondent mood. "I'm going to sell this place to the next person who walks through that door," he said. "For whatever they're willing to pay." Without hesitation, Nick emptied his pockets onto the bar. "Well," Nick said, "I've got seven dollars and thirty-two cents." His brother accepted, and for a handful of pocket change, Nick established himself in a lifelong career.

It would have been hard to find a spot in Mid-City where a bar had better odds of prospering. Across Tulane Avenue was the Dixie Brewery, whose employees were a predictably thirsty bunch, and a few blocks down on Perdido Street was the train depot for the Baton Rouge line. Travelers making their way along South Conti, particularly in the simmering summer months, inevitably ducked into Nick's for a glass of cool relief. Nick paid the train line a cumbersome homage on the sign out front, which read "Nick's Original Big Train Bar and Saloon."

Nick had a nearly paranoid fear that one day he might not have enough liquor on hand to meet demand. He was so panicked by the thought that he kept an enormous supply of extra hooch laid in, and he always kept the bar so amply stocked that making space for an extra bottle required some delicate rearranging. According to barroom lore, the overstock, in fact, spared the backbar in 1965, when Hurricane Betsy blew through New Orleans. The roof, pried off by high winds, nearly crushed the handcrafted backbar, but instead came to rest on the top shelf, whose tightly crammed bottles miraculously shouldered the load. In superstitious deference, Nick announced that the top shelf should never again be dusted, and today, a lush mantle of brown lint lies undisturbed on the bottles there.

Over the course of decades behind the bar, Nick made a name for himself as a skilled and innovative bartender, winning an international mixologists' competition twenty-three years in a row. His crowning achievement was that he could pour a 32-layer pousse-café parfait in a one-ounce glass. (The previous record was an 18-layer parfait.) The bar's menu still features many of Nick's concoctions. Management refuses to disclose any of the drinks' recipes, though their distinctive titles offer some suggestion of their effects. Some Nick named after the headlines of the day (e.g., "The Pearl Harbor," "The Mid-Atlantic Crisis"); others have baffling or ominous titles ("Underwater Demolition," "War Eagle," "Pregnant Canary"); and many have lewd, unappetizing names that do not bear reprinting.

Nick Castrogiovanni died in 1979, and supposedly he left such an oversupply of liquor that his wife, who took over, didn't have to buy a new bottle for several years. Today, Nick's grandson, Albert Kattine, owns the place, which these days tends to draw a mixed crowd of young neighborhood regulars and students from Tulane and Loyola Universities.

NAPOLEON IN THE NEW WORLD

In 1815, after Napoleon's defeat at Waterloo, Russian heads of state exiled the vanquished general to the island of St. Helena in the South Atlantic. Nicholas Girod, then mayor of New Orleans, admired Bonaparte, and with the help of the pirate Dominique You, Girod hatched a scheme to spring Napoleon from his island prison and spirit him back to New Orleans. One can only guess at the mayor's ambitions, but perhaps Girod envisioned New Orleans as a new seat of global power, with Napoleon at the helm and Girod himself as his lieutenant. Girod commissioned a fleet of ships for the voyage, and volunteered his own house at 500 Chartres Street to host the famous general. But on May 5, 1821, three days before the fleet was to depart, the conspiracy disintegrated — Napoleon had died of cancer on St. Helena, never to meet his ally in the New World.

Pascal's Manale Restaurant

1838 NAPOLEON AVENUE

at Dryades Street

MONDAY-FRIDAY 11:30AM-10PM

SATURDAY 4PM-10PM

☎ 504-895-4877

"**M**ANALE'S IS THE ONLY RESTAURANT WHERE THE CUSTOMER IS ALWAYS WRONG," THE LATE SENATOR F. EDWARD HÉBERT ONCE SAID OF THIS Uptown eatery. Pascal Radosta, who owned the restaurant for the better part of the twentieth century, was known around town as a bon vivant, a sportsman, and raconteur, but not as the sort of restaurateur who played to the whims of patrons.

"I would come in and order steak," Hébert said. "He would say, 'You're not going to get steak, you're going to eat oysters.' And so I ate oysters."

Radosta ran the restaurant as he pleased. If a customer whose looks he didn't like walked through the doors, Radosta would tell him, with the bar packed with patrons, "I'm sorry, but we're closed."

Radosta's uncle, a Sicilian named Frank Manale, started the business in 1913 on the site of a failing grocery at the corner of Napoleon and Dryades Streets. He called it simply "Manale Restaurant." Upon Frank Manale's death, Radosta took over. He added "Pascal's" to the sign out front, rechristening the restaurant with a name that continues to bewilder out-of-towners.

Under Pascal's hand, the bar became a rendezvous for sportsmen, political figures, civic leaders, and celebrities (the Marx Brothers, Joe DiMaggio, and Jack Dempsey have all darkened the door here). The barroom, windowless and dark as a ship's hold, is outfitted with barrelhead tables and wagonwheel lamps, which convey a comforting, refined rusticity. And while Pascal's is generally mentioned in the same breath with New Orleans's oldest and most estimable restaurants, its clientele has never been exclusively genteel. In the 1950s, the bar was a favorite nightspot of an off-duty policeman who, after a drink or two, would perform selections from operas popular in the day. During one recital, in a fit of heightened passion, he drew his gun in the crowded bar and accidentally fired off a round. Mortified, the officer fled, but the bullet remains lodged in the backbar today.

Pascal's menu consists of classic Italian dishes — pasta with meat sauce, veal Puccini, veal Marsala, veal parmigiana, fried eggplant, fried mozzarella — along with Creole standards: oysters Rockefeller and Bienville, gumbo, and fried soft-shell crabs. The signature item is the barbecued shrimp, a dish that appears on menus all over New Orleans but was pioneered here. The shrimp are enormous, cooked in a delicately spiced broth. Eating them involves some messy grappling (it cannot be done daintily), but at your request, the waiter will reach a well-scrubbed hand into your plate and demonstrate correct procedure for dismantling the crustaceans.

SNO-BALLS

New Orleanians care less about the passing of winter, spring, summer, and fall than they do the many gustatory seasons that come and go each year. Autumn is soft-shell crab season. Winter brings oysters. In spring, the air in the city turns pungent with crawfish boiling spices. But summer belongs to a man-made treat, the sno-ball.

The custom of eating sweetened snow supposedly began with the Roman Empire, but in New Orleans, the practice took off in 1934, when Ernest Hansen invented a device called "Hansen's Sno-Bliz." Sno-balls had been popular in New Orleans before Hansen's invention, but the Sno-Bliz, a motorized ice shaver, took the labor out of sno-ball preparation, which, in the pre-Hansen era, required a lot of hard work with a hand plane.

The uninitiated often confuse the sno-ball with the snow cone, which is common throughout the country but is sneered at in New Orleans. The chief difference between the two is the quality of a sno-ball's snow. It is shaved to a deliciously fine consistency and is far creamier than the crushed ice used in the sno-ball's granular cousin.

The ice is shaved from a hefty block, scooped into a paper cone and sweetened with the syrup of the customer's choosing. Most sno-ball shops keep fifty or more kinds of syrup on hand, ranging from common fruit flavors to piquant innovations such as orchid cream vanilla.

Sno-balls are sold at humble neighborhood stands and serving windows all across the city, though sno-ball aficionados generally swear allegiance to one of two titans of the local sno-ball scene: Plum Street Sno-Balls at 1300 Burdette Street in the Riverbend, or Hansen's Sno-Bliz Sweet Shop, which is still owned and operated by Ernest Hansen's family, at 4801 Tchoupitoulas Street. Despite their popularity, both shops heed seasonal tradition and close their doors from September to Easter.

Roman Candy

MAILING ADDRESS:

5510 CONSTANCE STREET

NEW ORLEANS, LA 70118

☎ 504-897-3937

HOLIDAYS IN THE CORTESE FAMILY WERE ALWAYS HERALDED BY A STICKY CULINARY RITUAL: LONG AFTERNOONS OF TAFFY-PULLING IN THE FAMILY kitchen. It hadn't occurred to Angelina Cortese, who had brought the recipe from her native Palermo, that folks might be willing to pay for the family treat. But her son Sam knew a marketable idea when he saw one. The young Cortese, a street vendor who sold fruit and vegetables from a horse-drawn wagon, started hawking his mother's candy along his route.

It sold well enough that in 1915, Sam Cortese decided to abandon the produce trade and peddle candy full-time. But Sam couldn't afford to lose a day's sales to stay home pulling taffy, so he began approaching local wheelwrights with a proposition: what he needed was a sort of rolling confectionery, a wagon with a functioning kitchen and windows all around — a feature generally reserved for hearses in those days. Also, Cortese had to be able to work the reins from inside the wagon, rather than from a driver's perch, so that he could make his taffy as the wagon bumped along the city streets. At first, Cortese couldn't find a wheelwright who wanted any part of his convoluted design. But ultimately he found one willing to take the project on, and together they built Cortese's roving kitchen, a wagon outfitted with marble cooling counters, an iron hook for pulling taffy, and a boisterous tugboat bell to announce the candy man's approach. Before the year was out, the Roman Candy wagon was open for business, appearing throughout New Orleans, in the suburbs of Chalmette and Metairie, and in Gretna, across the Mississippi River.

The recipe—corn syrup and sugar, cooked, cooled, pulled, and cut—stayed the same for the first twenty-five years or so, though in the 1940s, Cortese began experimenting with a variety of flavorings before settling on vanilla, strawberry, and chocolate. Sam Cortese stayed at the reins through the 1960s, and after his death in 1969, his grandson Ron Kotteman took command of the one-cart fleet. Kotteman still pulls the sweet, elastic skeins aboard his grandfather's wagon, which, cockeyed and rickety as it is, is still towed by mule over New Orleans's cratered boulevards. The wagon can be seen throughout the Central Business District and the French Quarter, but is most reliably found on St. Charles Avenue, near Audubon Park, when the weather is fine.

GIN FIZZ

2 OZ. GIN
JUICE OF 1/2 LEMON
1 TEASPOON POWDERED SUGAR
CARBONATED WATER

Combine gin, lemon juice, and sugar with ice and shake. Strain into a high-ball glass over ice, fill with carbonated water, and stir. A Silver Fizz is concocted with the addition of an egg white. In the 1880s, New Orleans bar owner Henry Ramos added orangeflower water and milk or cream to a Silver Fizz, creating what is now known as a Ramos Gin Fizz.

DIXIE BEER

The Dixie Brewing Company is still making beer in the original cypress barrels it used when it opened in 1907. In addition to traditional Dixie Beer, the brewery also produces Dixie Blackened Voodoo Lager, Dixie Crimson Voodoo Ale, and Dixie Jazz Amber Light. *Laissez les bon temps roulez!*

Sazerac Bar & Grill

123 BARONNE STREET

between Canal and Common Streets,

inside the Fairmont Hotel

DAILY 6AM-2PM, 5-10PM

☎ 800-527-4727

URING THE 1830s, CREOLE APOTHECARY ANTOINE AMEDEE PEYCHAUD OPER-
ATED A SMALL PHARMACY ON ROYAL STREET IN THE FRENCH QUARTER.
Peychaud spent his days mixing salves, tablets, and unguents, and in the
evenings he mixed drinks for a select few who gathered at the pharmacy after hours.
He served his drinks in an egg cup known in French as a *coquetier*. Those who didn't
speak fluent French called it a "cock-tay," and in the mouths of woozy patrons,
pronunciation blurred into a now familiar term—"cocktail."

The world's first so-called cocktail was a mixture of Peychaud's house-brewed
bitters and Sazerac-de-Forge et Fils brandy. Customers would later order the drink
under the simple title "Sazerac." The Sazerac quickly caught on in the city's coffee
houses (a euphemism for drinking establishments in Victorian New Orleans) and it
became a fashionable drink among New Orleans's elites. The Sazerac remains the
official libation of the Krewe of Rex, King of Mardi Gras.

In 1853, tavern owner Sewell Taylor dedicated his bar in Exchange Alley—the
Sazerac Coffee House—to the exclusive sale of Peychaud's cocktail. Bartenders
poured the drink for an upscale crowd of New Orleans politicians, gentry, and busi-
nessfolk. Women, however, were forbidden from the premises, except on one day a
year, Fat Tuesday, when New Orleans gentlewomen were invited to "storm" the
Sazerac Bar. "You couldn't get inside because of all the ladies," one frustrated
customer remarked.

At the turn of the century, the Sazerac moved from the French Quarter to the intersection of Gravier and Carondelet Streets, in the city's Central Business District. Prohibition dealt the bar a blow it never quite recovered from, and in 1949 the one-hundred-year old tavern closed its doors.

But soon after it closed, the bar was rescued by the Roosevelt Hotel and relocated to a spot on Baronne Street beside the Roosevelt's gilded main entrance. Seymour Weiss, the hotel's general manager, was more progressively minded than the Sazerac's earlier proprietors. When the bar reopened under his management, Weiss quashed the Sazerac's century-old prohibition against female customers, and women were "cordially invited at all times" to stop in for a drink.

In the late 1950s, the Sazerac moved to its current location, just off the hotel's lobby, replacing what was once the Roosevelt's "Main Bar." The bar benefits from the Main Bar's old furnishings: a 45-foot-long bar, rich walnut-paneled walls, and a gleaming art deco backbar, all crafted from the same African walnut tree.

The bar still serves New Orleans's best Sazerac cocktail, which, since 1870, has been made with rye instead of brandy, bitters, simple syrup, and a hint of the anise liquor Herbsaint. Bartenders here prepare them in dramatic style, which involves shaking free the excess anisette with an aerobatic toss of the glass.

The Fairmont chain of luxury hotels bought the Roosevelt in the 1950s, and added an adjacent restaurant, which serves breakfast, lunch, dinner, and (seasonally) a Sunday champagne brunch. The menu includes an excellent lobster bisque, stuffed trout, herb-crusted lamb chops, pecan crabcakes, and other Creole specialties.

THE ORIGINAL SAZERAC COCKTAIL

1 TEASPOON OF SIMPLE SYRUP
(OR 1 SUGAR CUBE OR 1 TEASPOON GRANULATED SUGAR)
3-4 DASHES PEYCHAUD BITTERS
2 OUNCES RYE WHISKEY
1/4 TEASPOON HERBSAINT
(OR PERNOD OR PASTIS)
STRIP OF LEMON PEEL

Fill a glass with ice. Pour the syrup or granulated sugar into a cocktail shaker, or, if using a sugar cube, moisten the sugar with a few drops of water and crush. Blend with rye and bitters. Add several ice cubes and stir. Discard the ice from the first glass and pour in the Herbsaint or Pernod and coat the inside of the entire glass, pouring out the excess. Strain the whiskey mixture into the glass coated with Herbsaint or Pernod. Twist the lemon peel over the glass so that the lemon oil drips into the drink, then rub the peel over the rim of the glass before serving.

Tortorici's

441 ROYAL STREET

at St. Louis Street

DAILY 5PM-10:30PM

☎ 504-522-4295

WHEN IT WAS LOUIS TORTORICI'S TURN TO PRESENT HIMSELF TO THE IMMI-GRATION CLERK AT THE PORT OF NEW ORLEANS, HE PRONOUNCED HIS name in the Sicilian manner, without belaboring the "i" at the end. The clerk handed Tortorici citizenship papers registering the name "Louis Tortorich." Louis had hopes of someday opening his own restaurant in the city, but he began his culinary career humbly, plucking chickens for a butcher in the French Market. Defeathering chickens, however, was not a very lucrative line, and Louis worried that his ambition to become a restaurateur might be permanently deferred. But he had the good fortune of marrying the daughter of a man of means, and in 1900, Louis opened a small eatery at the corner of Royal and St. Louis Streets.

With its menu of Sicilian dishes, its walls adorned with Italian flags and the coat of arms of the village where Tortorici was raised, the restaurant was an expatriate's tribute to his native land. Yet the sign out front bore not his family name but "Tortorich's," preserving the immigration clerk's mistake. It stayed that way until the 1960s, when Tortorici's grandsons, Anthony and Joseph, renovated the restaurant and proudly restored the Sicilian spelling to the menu and the sign over the door.

The Tortoricis ultimately sold the restaurant to the Karno family, who operate a number of restaurants and bars on Bourbon Street. Tortorici's still offers a full selection of Italian dishes — veal piccata, shrimp scampi, assorted antipasti, as well as an assortment of pastas — but the chefs give a nod to the local cuisine as well, with fried soft-shell crabs, barbecued shrimp, Louisiana trout pecan, seafood gumbo, crawfish étouffée, and other Cajun and Creole standbys.

Tortorici's also has an unpublicized attraction — a ghost named Rosie, who the staff claims haunts the deserted apartment above the restaurant and frequents the dining room as well. She has been known to materialize at the tables of patrons in mid-meal, and to frustrate the staff by pilfering the flatware. Little is known about her except that she goes out on Saturday nights, and returns on Sunday afternoons in a frolicsome mood.

A BOVE THE REAR DOOR TO TUJAGUE'S MAIN DINING ROOM HANGS A PHOTO-
GRAPH TAKEN IN THE BAR DURING PROHIBITION. A SINGLE GLASS SELTZER
bottle sits on the bar — there is no evidence of any liquor — yet a suspiciously
large staff of three bartenders stands by. Chances are slim that patrons were queuing
up for seltzer water.

Few New Orleans restaurants treated Prohibition with much reverence, but most
establishments at least made the pretense of serving their cocktails in a secluded rear
den. At Tujague's, waiters carried gin and bourbon bottles in their aprons and poured
highballs in heedless view of the entire house. Even after Repeal, Tujague's continued to flout local sumptuary laws, turning its briskest business on election days, when
taverns were obligated by law to lock their doors. Bartenders at Tujague's did, in fact,
keep the front doors locked, but they threw the rear entrance open, and from
morning to night, the bar was crammed with tippling politicians, awaiting returns
from the polls.

Guillaume Tujague and his wife, Marie Abadie, came to New Orleans in the
1850s, a golden era of antebellum prosperity in the city. Cotton and sugar prices were
high and crops were flourishing. The banks were thriving, coffers flush with revenue
from the booming ports. Tujague found work as a butcher in the French Market, and
after three years, in 1856, he'd stashed away sufficient savings to open a restaurant
in the old Spanish armory on Decatur Street. The Tujagues catered to the wharf
laborers, market workers, and seamen who crowded the riverfront, specializing in an

"early lunch"—seven courses of Creole dishes served during late morning, usually to men knocking off from the graveyard shift. The restaurant competed for trade with Madame Begue's, an unpretentious eatery a few doors up Decatur Street that had been serving French Quarter laborers and tradesmen since 1863. Before his death in 1912, Guillaume Tujague sold his restaurant to Phlibert Guichet, who soon annexed Madame Begue's and hung out a new sign bearing the late Tujague's name. Tujague's is now second in age only to Antoine's, and its interior has changed little over the years. There is still a scarcity of stools at the cypress bar, which is the oldest stand-up bar in the city. The ornate mirror that hangs above the rows of bottles arrived when the restaurant opened, more than 150 years ago (it graced a Paris bistro for ninety years before coming here), and the wall clock in the main dining room is the same one that rang in the turn of the twentieth century.

Tujague's still serves a six-course *table d'hôte* menu built around its original specialties: shrimp remoulade and boiled beef brisket with horseradish sauce. Other possibilities include stuffed shrimp, chicken bonne femme, and the daily seafood catch.

Uglesich Restaurant

1238 BARONNE STREET

between Erato and Clio Streets

MONDAY-FRIDAY 10:30AM-4PM

☎ 504-523-8571

I N THE RESTAURANT'S EARLY DAYS, IF YOU WERE IN SAM UGLESICH'S FAVOR HE DIDN'T BOTHER TO POUR YOUR DRINKS ONE GLASS AT A TIME. HE'D SET YOU UP with a fifth and a glass and trust you to reimburse him honestly when your paycheck came. Ducking the tab would have been easy enough, but in an age when social life revolved around the neighborhood restaurant, the prospect of being banned from Uglesich's was something nobody wanted to risk.

An immigrant from the island of Dugi Otok, off the coast of Croatia, Sam Uglesich had grown up among mariners and fishermen, people who drew their living from the sea. So when he opened his restaurant in 1924, it was seafood he sold: sandwiches or plates of fried shrimp, soft-shell crabs, trout, and oysters, likely harvested by fellow Yugoslavs who worked the oyster beds in Plaquemines Parish.

The restaurant first opened on South Rampart Street, two doors down from a club where Louis Armstrong played nightly gigs. Two years later, the restaurant moved to Central City, then a prosperous neighborhood, buoyed up by the surging fortunes of New Orleans's Jewish merchant class. The new building, a former saloon, was larger than the old address but it was still an unassuming place: a twenty-by-twenty-foot cottage across the street from Brown's Dairy. Sam Uglesich, with the help of his brother, his nephew, and his son, Anthony, worked the restaurant tirelessly, opening each morning at six, and shooing any loitering patrons off the barstools at 10pm. But as the neighborhood fell into decline through the '50s, '60s and '70s, much of the restaurant's local trade tapered off. After Sam Uglesich's death in the early

'70s, Anthony and his wife Gail cut the restaurant's hours to weekday lunches.

Although few of Uglesich's customers live in the neighborhood, the loss of its identity as a neighborhood eatery has been good for the bill of fare. The restaurant now offers a magnificent, though unfussy, roster of Creole-fusion dishes that have made Uglesich's one of the most successful lunch-only businesses in the country. Most days the front sidewalk is crowded with long lines of faithful locals and discriminating tourists.

The entire menu is excellent, but the waiter will urge you strongly to sample the specialties: fried green tomatoes topped with shrimp and remoulade sauce; fiery and tart shrimp Uggie, seasoned with three different chilies; barbecued shrimp sautéed in olive oil, basil, garlic, and parsley; pan-fried trout topped with a sauce of chicken stock, garlic, anchovies, and flayed jalapeños. No desserts, no coffee.

But for its revised menu, Uglesich's is still a pleasantly unvarnished, ramshackle room, with acoustical tile ceilings, a gray concrete floor, and a homely wood-laminate partition that separates the dining room from the tiny, harried kitchen. The restaurant has an extensive wine list, and mixes one of New Orleans's fiercer Bloody Marys but, closing at 4pm, Uglesich's does no saloon trade. There remains one customer for whom the owner says he'd still serve liquor on his father's honor system, but the man is in his upper nineties and he gave up drinking some time ago.

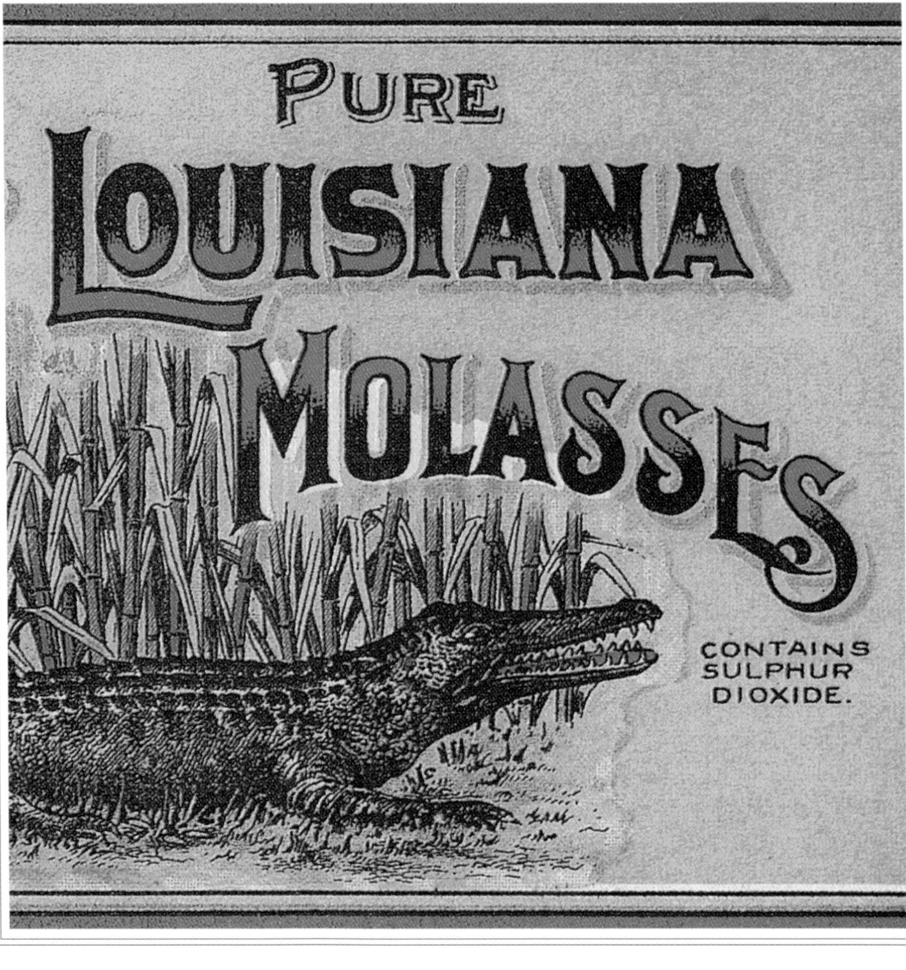
PURE
LOUISIANA
MOLASSES
CONTAINS
SULPHUR
DIOXIDE.

FOOD GLOSSARY

BOUDIN
Spicy sausage made with pork and rice.

BEIGNET
A square, powdered doughnut.

CAFÉ AU LAIT
Dark roasted coffee served with steamed milk.
Most New Orleans cafés make theirs with a chicory blend.

CHICORY
Roasted endive root, an additive in New Orleans-style coffee.

COURT-BOUILLON
Stew of poached fish (commonly redfish)
or other seafood and vegetables.

ÉTOUFFÉE
A slow-cooking method commonly used with crawfish.

FILÉ
Ground sassafras leaves, used as a thickener in gumbo.

GUMBO
Roux-based stew, made with seafood or sausage and chicken,
and either okra or filé powder.

GRILLADES
Meat served with tomato gravy and grits.

JAMBALAYA
Creole rice dish, usually cooked with sausage or shrimp,
tomatoes, onions, peppers, and spices.

MUFFULETTA
Sandwich of cold-cuts, cheeses, and olive salad served
on soft, round bread.

PO' BOY
Sandwich stuffed with fried seafood or cold cuts, served on French
bread. "Dressed" means with lettuce, tomato, and mayonnaise.

REMOULADE
A seafood sauce made with horseradish, ketchup, and
a variety of spices.

ROUX
Flour slow-cooked in hot butter or oil. A well-made roux has a pleasant,
nutty aroma and is the base ingredient in gumbo and other soups.

TASSO
Dry cured pork shoulder used as a seasoning meat.

SHOPS

Bennett's Camera and Video

WHEN PHOTOGRAPHY BEGAN CATCHING ON IN NEW ORLEANS, SHOPPING AT BENNETT'S COULD BE A DEADLY BUSINESS. ONE YEAR, AROUND THE HOLIdays, when the store was crowded with clamoring customers, the strain was too much for one shopper who suffered a heart attack and expired on the shop floor. The other patrons were unmoved and simply stepped over the body to fill in the empty spot at the counter.

Photography was still an unusual hobby when Joseph Bennett opened his small photographic shop in 1909 on lower St. Charles Avenue. Joseph Bennett did meager sales in sheet film, wooden view cameras with leather bellows, box cameras, processing chemicals, and flash powder, but he shored up his business with a selection of gifts: gift cards, stationery, hairbrush sets. By the 1920s, a growing community of photo enthusiasts kept the store busy, and Bennett scaled back on his inventory of gift shop wares. In the '50s and '60s, Bennett's sold Super 8 equipment to New Orleanians eager to capture trips abroad or life at home in moving portraits. Now, patrons return to Bennett's with crates of dusty Super 8 reels to have those same home movies transferred to video or DVD.

In the 1970s, the oil market declined and many of the petrochemical companies that had tenanted the downtown skyscrapers left town, which turned the Central Business District into a desolate place. Bennett's also left, for Metairie, moving first to Severn and 15th Street, and then in 1989, to its current location on Severn and 18th.

Bourbon French Parfums

815 ROYAL STREET

between St. Ann and Dumaine Streets

DAILY 9AM-5PM

☎ 504-522-4480

IN 1843, PERFUMER AUGUST DOUSSAN ARRIVED FROM PARIS AND ESTABLISHED BOURBON FRENCH PARFUMS. HE BROUGHT ALONG HIS SIGNATURE FRAGRANCE, "Kus Kus"—a spicy, tropical aroma that became an immediate favorite among the Creole ladies. When it came time to retire, Doussan left New Orleans to live out his years in the Caribbean. Travelers who later sailed to Haiti and Jamaica were surprised to catch the scent of Doussan's Kus Kus among local women, evidence that Doussan had continued perfuming well into old age. His successor, J.H. Tyndall, made his name as the exclusive American retailer of the famous fragrance Eau de Cologne, used by Napoleon. During the Civil War, Tyndall also sold "perfume buttons"—silver buttons wrought around absorbent fabric. A soldier's wife or mother would snip a scented button from her dress and sew it to the young man's collar as a memento of home.

Marguerite Caro took over at the turn of the last century. Her granddaughter contributed the perfume "Voodoo Love"—a recreation of a fragrant potion supposedly used by nineteenth-century voodoo priestess Marie Laveau. Voodoo Love's active ingredient is vetiver, a bayou weed native to Louisiana. In plantation homes, servants would dry the aromatic roots of the stalky grass and lay them out in front of open windows to sweeten the summer winds blowing through the house. The plant is a longstanding favorite of sachet makers, and also of the Louisiana Soil Conservation Service, which sows vetiver in Delta marshlands to keep the swamp floor from washing out. Today, Mary Behler runs the shop, and still sells Kus Kus and other fragrances, which she mixes herself in the store's backroom.

[132]

Coleman E. Adler & Sons, Inc.

722 CANAL STREET

between Carondelet Street and St. Charles Avenue

MONDAY-SATURDAY 10:30AM-5:30PM

☎ 504-523-5292

IN THE OPENING PASSAGE OF JOHN KENNEDY TOOLE'S *CONFEDERACY OF DUNCES*, DISAPPROVING MISFIT IGNATIUS J. REILLY STANDS IN THE CROWD under the clock in front of the D.H. Holmes department store, waiting impatiently for his mother to appear. For a century or so, Canal Street was the city's humming retail center, where New Orleanians could pass the better part of a day browsing the shops that lined the wide boulevard. At the end of the outing, husbands, wives, and children, like Ignatius and his mom, inevitably had plans to rendezvous under the clock at D.H. Holmes.

Most of the shops of Canal Street's heyday have since moved out to suburban malls or closed their doors, as D.H. Holmes did in 1988. These days, there's only one significant clock on Canal Street, the wrecking-ball-sized timepiece affixed to the awning in front of Coleman E. Adler & Sons.

Coleman Adler got his start in retail as a "jobber," traveling throughout the Gulf South, selling a variety of merchandise to stores along his route. Coleman's travels displeased his girlfriend, who said she'd marry him if he hung up his valise and opened a shop in town, which he did in 1898.

Adler's shop began modestly, but over the years expanded to an entire city block, offering an inventory in the tradition of Tiffany & Co.— jewelry, silver, china, crystal, and a variety of gift items. Over its long history, the store has handled commissions for several U.S. Presidents. It is the exclusive jeweler for New Orleans's oldest carnival krewes, and the keeper of the crown jewels for Rex, King of Mardi Gras.

Ed Smith's Stencil Works

326 CAMP STREET

between Perdido and Gravier Streets

MONDAY-FRIDAY 7:30AM-4:30PM

☎ 504-525-2128

WHEN THE CIVIL WAR ENDED, ED SMITH OF BALTIMORE JOINED THE WAVE OF VENTURESOME NORTHERNERS (KNOWN TO SOME AS "CARPETBAGGERS") setting out in search of riches in the war-ravaged South. But Smith, a gaunt man with a beard that reached his sternum, hardly fit the profile of the Yankee swank. Smith arrived in New Orleans and established himself in an obscure specialty: manufacturing "log hammers," which were steel mallets fitted with dies for marking and grading rough timber. It was an oddly profitable line of work. Southern cities were in a frenzy tending their war wounds with new construction, and the timber business boomed on the Mississippi's west bank where cypress trees still stood in thick groves. The trees toppled by the thousands, and before each log was shipped out, a timberman marked it with one of Ed Smith's hammers.

Smith soon started manufacturing other products: die-cut stencils, stamps, and seals—dutiful but unnoticed items which no one else in town was making at the time. His stencils were often simple and utilitarian: large, frank letters to brand a ship's hull, or crisp scripts for the sides of soda crates. But Smith's shop also made brass and copper stencils of breathtaking craft and intricacy. Several hang in the shop today: Hercules tackling the Nimean lion, the Capitol building, and a beautiful old sign for the shop's own storefront.

Ed Smith's shop, through a tortuous circuit of inheritances, remains in the family today, and still makes stencils using dies dating back to the turn of the last century. Smith's is the exclusive manufacturer of the star-and-crescent badges worn by New

Orleans police officers, and makes most of the official seals of New Orleans's notary publics. Smith's also arranges the forging of the brass historic markers that appear in nearly every line of sight in the French Quarter. The shop recently had an order from a chef in Honolulu who wanted to stencil his dessert plates with patterns in powdered sugar — a delicate request for a shop that got its start making tools for banging dents in logs.

H. Rault Locksmiths

LESS, SADLY, IS KNOWN ABOUT THE LIFE OF HENRY RAULT THAN HOW HE MET HIS END. RAULT, WHO HAD ESTABLISHED HIS LOCKSMITH SHOP IN 1845, LIVED most of his life in an era when one didn't bother looking both ways before stepping off the curb. But one afternoon, at the age of ninety-two, Rault was crossing Magazine Street, en route to New Orleans's latest amusement, the motion picture matinee, when his fate collided with another new technology, the Model T Ford.

Rault's locksmith shop had its first location in the French Quarter, though it later moved to the Garden District, first to 3013 Magazine Street, and then a few doors down to 3027 Magazine, which the business acquired in 1926 for $9,000. As the years wore on, owners of aging Uptown mansions began visiting the shop in search of authentic replacements for broken or exhausted hardware, and H. Rault turned its business exclusively toward antiques and restoration.

In 1992, Russell Staub, the fourth generation of Henry Rault's descendants, sold the shop along with the building to a man named Jim Miller. The shop had suffered in recent years, not least from Staub's hobbies as a blood-sport enthusiast. The back yard held pens for pit-bulls, and the second floor had been converted to a coop for fighting cocks.

After an application of fresh clapboards and extensive scrubbing, H. Rault's hardly looks worse for the spell of neglect. Today, the small showroom holds a display of nineteenth-century safes, bit keys, ornamental rim locks, and in the back room, a cabinet of locks and ignition parts to fit ancient automobiles, including the Model T.

PRONUNCIATION KEY:

TCHOUPITOULAS (STREET): *chop-a-TOO-lus*

BURGUNDY (STREET): *bur-GUN-dee*

CHARTRES (STREET): *CHART-ers*

MELPOMENE (STREET): *MEL-po-mean*

TERPSICHORE (STREET): *TERP-si-core*

CALLIOPE (STREET): *CALLY-ope*

VIEUX CARRÉ: *voo-ka-RAY*

BEIGNET: *ben-YAY*

PRALINE: *PRAH-leene*

LAGNIAPPE: *LAN-yap*

COURT-BOUILLON: *COO-bee-yon*

TUJAGUE'S (RESTAURANT): *TWO-jacks*

NEW ORLEANS: *new OR-lee-uns, N'AW-lins or new OR-luns; never new or-LEENS*

Harry's Hardware

3535 MAGAZINE STREET

at Foucher Street

MONDAY-SATURDAY 8AM-7PM,

SUNDAY 9AM-5PM

☎ 504-896-1500

PEOPLE IN THE NEIGHBORHOOD AROUND 326 SOUTH RAMPART STREET KNEW THAT IN A SPELL OF HARD LUCK, THEY COULD KNOCK ON THE BACK DOOR AT Harry Offner's hardware store, and the proprietor would usually help out with a short-term loan, or a free meal of whatever he had on hand. In the worst of times, like the hard years of the Depression, Offner had more people knocking at his hardware store's back door than were coming through the front entrance.

Offner came to America from Austria in the waning years of the nineteenth century, when he was thirteen years old. He landed at Ellis Island and then made his way to New Orleans, where a brother of his was struggling to establish himself in the hardware business. When Harry Offner opened his own store in 1907, it was his reputation as a generous businessman and compassionate neighbor that helped make the place a success. It was a simple business, selling nails, nuts and bolts, roofing supplies, and basic tools to the carpenters and construction workers who lived nearby. The inventory here was reliable and unvarying, with a single seasonal item: ice skates during the winter holidays.

When he was thirty-two, Offner married nineteen-year-old Celia Covert, a New Yorker whose parents had come to New Orleans to open a shoe store on South Rampart Street, then a lively neighborhood inhabited mostly by Jewish immigrants. Though the store was doing well, the Offners and their five children lived in a modest apartment above the shop. It was Harry's attitude that if there was food on the table and a roof overhead, the rest could go to the folks lining up daily at his shop's back door, or to charitable organizations around town.

His children worked alongside him at the store, and Harry held them to a single workplace rule: never try to chase down a shoplifter. This was a privilege reserved for Harry himself, who would dash out from behind the counter every time a thief made a break for it.

In the years after Offner's death in 1951, his daughters and sons-in-law closed the shop and reopened a branch on Magazine Street. Harry's now has four locations and sells everything you'd expect to find at a well-stocked hardware store.

Herwig's Bicycle Store

5924 MAGAZINE STREET

between Eleonore and State Streets

TUESDAY-FRIDAY 9:30AM-5PM

SATURDAY 9:30AM-3:30PM

☏ 504-897-2311

N O SHOP IN NEW ORLEANS IN THE 1920s COULD EXPECT TO STAY IN BUSINESS WITHOUT AN ACTIVE PLATOON OF DELIVERYMEN, BUT AUTOMOBILES WERE still exorbitant luxuries for most citizens. So most things money could buy arrived at the customer's door in the cargo basket of a bicycle.

In 1928, Ernest Herwig opened his shop on the ground floor of a raised, double-shotgun house on upper Magazine Street, between Eleonore and State Streets. Herwig quickly had his hands full, tending to the fleets of delivery cycles across the city. Bicycles in those days had heavy steel frames and high-pressure, tubeless tires cemented to thick wooden rims. The wheels, in particular, fared poorly on New Orleans's rugged gravel streets and the glue had a way of decaying in the glaring Louisiana sunlight, so even when Herwig wasn't selling new models, a profitable and unceasing epidemic of blown tires kept the cash register chiming.

When the Depression hit, even the relatively modest $20 or $30 sticker price on Herwig's bikes was beyond many people's means, so he added a rental business at the shop: fifteen cents an hour, or two hours for a quarter. On weekends, when people would treat themselves to an afternoon of cycling through the shade of live oaks in Audubon Park, the store was mobbed, often bringing in $75 or more in rental fees over the course of an afternoon.

When Herwig wasn't busy with customers, he was banging around in the back of the shop, toiling after a private obsession — a water-faring cycle. In 1933, Herwig

patented a working prototype—a mammoth aquatic tricycle buoyed up by three galvanized steel paddlewheel-pontoons. Herwig had ambitions of moving one day to Florida and earning a living renting his inventions, but the plan never materialized. Yet the water bikes were something of a sensation—MovieTone News came to down to film Herwig's son Stanley pedaling one on Lake Pontchartrain, and a pair of brave female volunteers successfully rode the cycles across the lake to Mandeville, a voyage of twenty-seven miles.

After World War II, Ernest's son, Ernest Herwig Jr., joined the business, and ran it until 1991, when it passed to his nephew. The store is still at Eleonore and Magazine, and sells bicycles and cycling accessories.

Hurwitz Mintz

211 ROYAL STREET

between Iberville and Bienville Streets

MONDAY, THURSDAY 10AM-9PM

TUESDAY-WEDNESDAY, FRIDAY 10AM-6PM

SATURDAY 10AM-8PM; SUNDAY 10AM-7PM

☎ 504-568-9555

IN THE 1920s, WHEN NEW ORLEANIANS WENT SHOPPING FOR FURNITURE, ODDS WERE THAT THEY'D VISIT A STORE WITH THE MINTZ NAME STENCILED ON THE window. There was Mintz Furniture, Mintz and Mintz, Mintz-Hurwitz, and Hurwitz-Mintz. But of all the Mintz concerns, only the latter, Hurwitz-Mintz, endured.

Morris Mintz came to Louisiana in the teens from Cabrin, Belarussia, a town whose nationality drifted between Poland and the Soviet Union almost seasonally. He found work, as many immigrants did, as a door-to-door salesman, selling catalogue items to people along his Westwego route. Morris had spent his childhood in Cabrin around his father's lumber mill. Watching wood being planed and milled had stirred in Morris an interest in furniture and woodcraft. And so, in 1923, when he'd saved a decent sum from his catalogue route, he teamed up with a man named Joseph Hurwitz and opened shop at 211 Royal Street. Competition was fierce, particularly from Morris's fellow Mintzes. The Mintzes would ruthlessly cut prices on one another during business hours, but at night the families would convene for meals, their affection for each other no worse for the day's stern dealings.

In 1982, the Mintz family bought out the Hurwitz family's interest, but left the name unchanged. Mitchell Mintz, Morris's grandson, runs the business today.

Ida Manheim Antiques

403-409 ROYAL STREET

between Conti and St. Louis Streets

MONDAY-SATURDAY 9AM-5PM

☎ 504-620-4114

EARLY IN THE TWENTIETH CENTURY, AT THE AGE OF THIRTEEN, BERNARD MANHEIM SET OUT FROM HIS NATIVE AUSTRIA TO LEARN SOMETHING OF THE furniture trade. He went first to London, and spent two years as an apprentice to a cabinetmaker, but he soon decided to try his hand at dealing antiques. At eighteen, he traveled to New York. He spent a scant few weeks taking in the city and quickly realized that Manhattan had no shortage of antiques dealers. So he came south to New Orleans, then the second largest seaport in the United States, and opened an antique gallery and a small cabinet shop in 1919 in the Vieux Carré at 403 Royal Street.

But the sorts of items being bought and sold in New Orleans were a disappointment to Manheim, who had whetted his own interests in antique furniture while browsing the vast collections of London firms. The stores of period furniture that had once furnished the mansions and plantation homes along the Mississippi had been scattered or sold off during the Civil War, and Manheim had a hard time finding quality pieces more than a few decades old. So he began traveling back to his native Europe, returning with period French and English furniture, Dutch grandfather clocks, ancient Chinese porcelains, bronze and marble statuary, and a renowned assortment of jade. Manheim's collection quickly became one of the largest and most comprehensive in the city. Today, Ida Manheim Antiques specializes in seventeenth-, eighteenth-, and nineteenth-century European art and furniture.

Keil's Antiques

THE PROPRIETORS OF KEIL'S ANTIQUES HAVE ALWAYS BELIEVED THAT NOTHING—NEITHER THE ITEMS THEY SELL, NOR THE PEOPLE WHO HELP sell them—ever really outlives its usefulness. The store's porter, Benjamin Hensley, has been helping out at Keil's for seventy-eight years and still comes to work here every morning. Eddie Trittel has been restoring furniture and crystal upstairs in the Keil's workshop since the 1950s. Margaret Keil, who ran the business with her husband Morris for much of the twentieth century, was still making buying trips to Paris when she was ninety years old.

Margaret began working at Keil's when she was only fifteen, as an assistant to Hermina Keil, an immigrant from Alsace-Lorraine, who had opened the shop in 1899. It wasn't long before Margaret fell in love with Morris Keil, Hermina's son. It was an ideal match. Morris, who didn't share his wife's passion for travel, would make sketches of items he wanted for the shop, and Margaret, who spoke fluent French, would head off to Europe to buy. Margaret's travels engendered a rich and storied life. She stood among cheering Parisians when Lindbergh completed his transatlantic flight. Three decades later she was a passenger on the *Andrea Doria* when it sank off the coast of Nantucket.

Today, Margaret Keil's daughter and grandchildren, Peter and Keil Moss, manage the store, which houses an eclectic stock of eighteenth- and nineteenth-century French and English artwork, furniture, and jewelry, as well as a sparkling firmament of Waterford and Baccarat chandeliers.

Laura's Candies

331 CHARTRES STREET

between Conti and Bienville Streets

DAILY 10AM-5:30PM

☎ 504-525-3880

938 ROYAL STREET

at St. Philip Street

DAILY 9:30AM-5:30PM

☎ 504-524-9259

IN THE NINETEENTH CENTURY, ONE OF THE FEW OPPORTUNITIES OPEN TO FREED WOMEN OF COLOR IN NEW ORLEANS WAS SELLING REFRESHMENTS TO passersby from curbside stands at street corners in the French Quarter. Tabletops creaked under the weight of gumbo crocks; platters of *calas tout chaud*, fried rice cakes sweetened with honey (now nearly disappeared from the local diet); bottles of spruce beer; and plates of pralines — which share a place in New Orleans's culinary canon with gumbo and red beans and rice.

In 1913, Laura Watson opened her praline shop, the oldest remaining confectionery in New Orleans, at 115 Royal Street. Little is known about the shop's history, only that it passed from Laura to her daughter Jeanine, who then sold it to a Mrs. Crawford in the 1960s. Crawford packaged and sold a range of confections under the name "Vieux Carré." Another of Crawford's trademarks was a music box whose sole tune, "On the Battlefield," broadcast onto Royal Street in an unending cycle. "On the Battlefield" was not beloved by the staff, but it had a Pavlovian effect on passersby, who lined up on the sidewalk for a taste of Vieux Carré's sugary goods.

In 1997, chocolatier John Dutton bought the store and restored Laura's name to its labels. Some New Orleans confectioners emulsify their pralines with cream or milk, but Laura's still sells the traditional version, made only with sugar, water, and pecans, cooked and then cooled on a marble slab. This recipe makes for a grainier treat, but one that does not melt in hot weather.

WHEN MENDEL S. RAU CAME TO NEW ORLEANS IN 1908 HE WAS PLEASED TO FIND WORK AT A USED FURNITURE STORE, BUT HE KNEW HE WOULDN'T GET far on his salary of eleven dollars a week. Eventually, he struck out on his own and, with $250 in savings, established a small antique shop on Royal Street. Rau spent long weeks on the road, traveling by bus as far as New England, combing second-hand stores for undiscovered rarities. The shop grew, owing in large part to Rau's stern approach to business. "If you took a dollar out of your pocket and said you'd sell it to him for seventy-five cents, he'd offer you fifty," said Bill Rau, Mendel Rau's grandson, and the shop's current owner.

With a 25,000 square-foot showroom, M.S. Rau is the largest antiques dealer in New Orleans, and its collection of antiques and objets d'art have earned the store international renown. The main showroom holds, among other things, a wide collection of cut glass (of which M.S. Rau is the oldest dealer in the United States), furniture, porcelain, music boxes, canes, sculpture, and paintings. Serious collectors might be invited for a tour behind the false wall in the rear of the showroom that opens on to a warren of exquisite curiosities. The centerpiece of Rau's exclusive collection is the Chevy Chase sideboard, a piece of carved oak depicting scenes from a fifteenth-century Scottish battle. It took a Victorian woodcarver six years to complete the piece. An outrageously impractical piece of furniture, the sideboard sells for $750,000, and there are few doorways in the world it could fit through; yet it's difficult to look straight at it and not go dizzy with awe.

Meyer the Hatter

120 ST. CHARLES AVENUE

between Canal and Common Streets

MONDAY-SATURDAY 10AM-5:45PM

☎ 504-525-1048

T THE TURN OF THE TWENTIETH CENTURY, MEN NEEDED HATS FOR ALL OCCASIONS AND EVERY SEASON, AND MEYER'S STAYED BUSY YEAR ROUND. IN Louisiana's scant cold months, men came to the shop for sturdy Homburgs, derbies, and top hats. In the summer, they came for stiff straw boaters to spend the hot months in a portable diameter of shade.

The shop's founder, Samuel H. Meyer, got his start at a nearby clothing store, making deliveries to clients around town, and brushing and fussing over the inventory of fine hats at the shop. Meyer took pleasure in the work, and his employers took note. "You like hats so much," they said, "you ought to open up your own store." And in 1894, with a $500 loan from his wife, Meyer opened a small shop on St. Charles Avenue. The Stetson sales representative knew Meyer from his previous job and had enough faith in the young merchant to guarantee his first order. Meyer's still sells Stetson hats today and holds the second oldest account on Stetson's books. In the Jim Crow era, Meyer the Hatter was the only shop in town that let its African-American customers try on the merchandise. "There was a practical reason," said Sam Meyer, the founder's grandson. "You can't sell somebody a hat if they can't try it on." Incidentally, none of the shop's less progressive competitors are around today. "We outlasted everybody," Meyer said. "They're either bankrupt or they're dead."

Meyer's claims to be the largest hatter in the South, though it hardly feels that way when you set foot in the shop — a single oblong room where customers do their shopping between seemingly collapsing walls of boxed inventory.

Peter A. Chopin Florist

3138 MAGAZINE STREET

between Harmony and 9th Streets

MONDAY-FRIDAY 8AM-5PM

SATURDAY 8AM-4PM

☎ 504-891-4455

WHEN PETER CHOPIN'S FATHER DIED, IN 1894, HE LEFT HIS FAMILY $49, A HORSE AND WAGON, A LIMITED COLLECTION OF GARDENING TOOLS, AND $4,000 in debts and obligations. Chopin was only seventeen years old, but the duty of supporting his mother and four siblings fell to him. He began his career where his father had left off, tending to the lawns and flowerbeds of wealthy citizens of the Garden District and Uptown neighborhoods. These were uncertain years for the Chopin family. Peter struggled to stay in business, even as his family endured evictions from a series of apartments. He worked ceaselessly, and in time he'd saved enough to open a florist's shop at Magazine and 8th Streets. He sold a vivid array of flowers — lilies of the valley, football chrysanthemums, sweet peas, gladiolas, peonies, carnations, roses — and delivered floral arrangements with the horse and wagon his father had left him.

Chopin grew to be one of New Orleans's best-respected florists and was regularly hired for events at the Governor's mansion in Baton Rouge. And though it was an occupation he came to by necessity, Chopin acquired a romantic regard for floral work. Upon retiring, he wrote, "As long as the human heart is capable of love, friendship, esteem and sympathetic expression, just that long will the services of the florist be needed to give material expression to these tender sentiments of the soul." His granddaughter Elizabeth runs Peter Chopin's today at 3138 Magazine Street.

LAGNIAPPE

Lagniappe is a word used throughout southern Louisiana by merchants to describe a small gift given to customers in addition to the customer's purchase.

In *Life on the Mississippi*, published in 1883, Mark Twain defined lagniappe: "We picked up one excellent word—a word worth traveling to New Orleans to get; a nice limber, expressive, handy word—'lagniappe.' They pronounce it lanny-*yap*...The custom originated in the Spanish quarter of the city. When a child or a servant buys something in a shop—or even the mayor or the governor, for aught I know—he finishes the operation by saying 'Give me something for lagniappe'. The shopman always responds; gives the child a bit of licorice-root, gives the servant a cheap cigar or a spool of thread, gives the governor—I don't know what he gives the governor; support, likely."

Rapp's Luggage and Gifts

604 CANAL STREET

at Camp Street

MONDAY-SATURDAY 9:30AM-5:30PM

☎ 504-552-4262

GEORGE RAPP, WHO CAME TO THE STATES FROM USTICA, GERMANY, JUST AS THE CIVIL WAR WAS WINDING DOWN, HAD HOPES OF MAKING A LIVING IN New Orleans as an accountant. He found work easily enough (it's not known where) but his aptitude for the work didn't quite match his enthusiasm, and soon after he got the job, he was dismissed. He didn't let it dismay him, and he instead pursued a career in luggage retail and repair. In 1865, he purchased Mack's Trunk Store on Common Street, moving it eventually to the bustling retail corridor of lower Canal Street and ultimately putting his own name on the sign. As transatlantic steamship travel came into vogue with New Orleans's wealthier set, travelers came to Rapp's to equip themselves with steamer trunks and other voyaging necessities. Rapp also did a heavy trade in hatboxes, suitcases, sealskin wallets, and other luggage, most of which were available in only a narrow spectrum of colors. "You can have any color you like," ran Rapp's unofficial slogan, "as long as it's black or brown."

Rapp retired in the 1920s, and his son-in-law Anton Tranchina abandoned his dental practice to take over the shop. George Rapp Tranchina, Jr., George Rapp's great grandson, owns the business today. Still at its Canal Street address, the shop carries popular luggage brands, as well as a broad selection of wallets, clocks, and other travel accessories.

Rolland Safe and Lock

1926 AIRLINE DRIVE

by Labarre Road

MONDAY-FRIDAY 8AM-5PM

☎ 504-835-7233

WHEN LUCIEN ROLLAND WAS IN THE FOURTH GRADE, HE DECIDED HE'D PREFER LOCKSMITHING TO STUDYING, AND, IN THE FIRST YEARS OF THE twentieth century, he abandoned school to begin his career. Rolland bought himself a set of files and set up a table, strangely, in a sandwich shop in the 200 block of Magazine Street. Diners would hand him keys they wanted copied and by the time they'd finished eating he would have filed down the duplicates. The keys, of course, were simpler then — blocky, skeleton keys that made for easy copying. Locks operated on an unexacting lever mechanism that tended to forgive whatever spare burrs and imperfections Rolland's young, inexpert hands failed to plane away.

The proprietors of H. Rault Locksmiths noticed Rolland's talents, and hired him away from his grinding table, though he worked for Rault only a short while before World War I took him overseas. He made it home in one piece, and in 1918 opened a shop at 245 Magazine Street, not far from the sandwich store where he'd started.

Wars have an interesting effect on the locksmithing trade: after any armistice, many of the foundries and machine shops previously busy manufacturing ordnance turn their attentions to building better locks. Not long after World War I, the old skeleton keys and lever mechanisms began to disappear, giving way to the pin-and-tumbler system modern locks use today. Rolland's business grew with the new technology, and as the automobile age got underway, he purchased a fleet of canary yellow Austin Minis for his staff to take on house calls. "The Big Lock Company with the Midget Automobiles," read a slogan on the Minis' doors.

NEW ORLEANS ATHLETIC CLUB

222 NORTH RAMPART STREET

North Rampart between Iberville and Bienville Streets

MONDAY-FRIDAY 5:30-10AM;

SATURDAY-SUNDAY 8-6PM

☎ 504-525-2375

O N SEPTEMBER 2, 1872, JACINTO C. ALEIX AND A GROUP OF THIRTEEN FRIENDS GOT TOGETHER AND BUILT A CRUDE SET OF PARALLEL bars on a patch of ground behind Aleix's house on Esplanade Avenue. It wasn't the most impressive set-up, but the group agreed to meet here regularly, calling themselves the Independent Gymnastic Club. Without so much as four walls to house his new institution, Aleix ceremoniously drafted a constitution for the club. Its objective, he wrote, was to promote good health "by sufficient gymnastic exercise." The charter included Aleix's mandate that the club's rolls never exceed 14 people, and that members must be "over 16 years of age and under 35, of a good moral character and gentlemanly deportment and have no deformity."

Demand quickly persuaded Aleix to expand membership, and within two years, the club — now with 50 members — moved indoors, to an undistinguished building at Rampart and Bienville Streets that had once been used to stable circus elephants. The floors of the club were hard-packed soil, strewn with sawdust. The club's modest gymnasium was lit with smoggy oil lamps. The place had no hot water, and at the end of an afternoon's exertions, athletes bathed themselves with a garden hose in halved wine casks. By 1884, the club had attracted 350 dues-paying members, and was sufficiently flush to move to quarters more suitable for young New Orleans gentlemen. In 1890, the club bought the Mastich mansion on Rampart Street and constructed a new gymnasium behind it. The cornerstone was set in place in 1891 by member Edward D. White, who later became Chief Justice of the Supreme Court under the Taft administration.

The club still occupies the Rampart Street premises, whose graceful interiors are very distant indeed from Jacinto Aleix's backyard on Esplanade Avenue. In the front exercise room, a battery of elliptical trainers strikes a peculiar note with the crystal chandelier, the parquet floors, and marble fireplace. The club boasts an elegant library, redolent of chlorine and old oak; a pleasant barroom — Vaughan's Pub — with an exquisite mahogany backbar; a main workout room with white columns and blonde brick; and a skylit natatorium in an echoing atrium of marble and wrought iron.

The club has a jogging track, a basketball court, as well as facilities for weightlifting, boxing, cardiovascular training, and racquet sports. Over the years, the club has attracted a number of celebrated members. The notorious governors Huey and Earl Long both belonged, along with many of the city's most prominent businessmen and politicians. Actor Johnny Weismuller once swam in the club's pool, and heavyweight boxing champion John L. Sullivan trained here for his seventy-four-round bare-knuckle bout with Jake Kilrain in 1889. A plaster cast of the famous pugilist's arm rests in a glass case in the lobby.

Royal Pharmacy

1101 ROYAL STREET

at Ursulines Street

MONDAY-SATURDAY 9AM-5:30PM

☏ 504-523-5401

BELOW THE WORN, SILVER LETTERING IN THE WINDOW OF THE ROYAL PHARMACY IS A PALE NEON SIGN READING "SODA FOUNTAIN" IN LUMINOUS BLUE script. The sign is one of the only details here that smacks of recent renovation, and it regularly lures in parched patrons who are dismayed to learn that the soda fountain hasn't worked in years. The fountain is a charming relic of green marble and worn chrome — "Too expensive to fix and too pretty to get rid of," says Kevin Tusa, the current owner and pharmacist.

Tusa's father, Charles Tusa, purchased the pharmacy in 1938 from Lewis Castillon, who had opened the business in the late 1890s. The shop's pressed tin ceilings, stamped with New Orleans's trademark fleur-de-lis, date back to its first days, as do the tile floors. The shelves still hold popular curatives from the pharmacy's distant past, including "flour sulfur" and "phospho-lecithin with strychnine."

The pharmacy came of age in a rougher era in the French Quarter's history. In 1927, just around the corner, a murder of local renown was committed, in which a local butcher dismembered his wife and sister-in-law. The scene was grisly, and police discovered the disquieting detail that the woman's wedding ring had been tucked into a wound in her back. Had the women lived, they would surely have been taken to the Royal Pharmacy, where a rotation of doctors kept regular office hours.

As the neighborhood grew more prosperous, the clientele improved, and included Tennessee Williams, who visited often to have his prescriptions filled.

Rubenstein Bros.

102 ST. CHARLES AVENUE

at Canal Street

MONDAY-THURSDAY 10AM-5:45PM

FRIDAY-SATURDAY 10AM-6PM

☎ 504-581-6666

WHEN MORRIS RUBENSTEIN ASKED HIS GIRLFRIEND'S PARENTS FOR THEIR DAUGHTER'S HAND, THEY ANSWERED THAT THEY'D GIVE THEIR BLESSING as soon as he'd landed a paying job. But jobs weren't easy to come by in New Orleans in the 1920s, so Rubenstein decided to give himself one, and he opened a tiny haberdashery in an eleven-by-fourteen storefront at the intersection of Canal Street and St. Charles Avenue. Morris soon brought his brother, Elkin, into the business, and the Rubensteins made a living selling shirts, collars, and neckties to New Orleans gentlemen.

The Rubensteins had little experience in the clothing business, and when their first customer to purchase a full suit asked to have the pants altered, Morris and Elkin looked at one another helplessly, but told the customer to return next week. When the man came back for his suit, the suit hadn't yet been fixed. The brothers then told the customer it would be just a little while longer, but they still hadn't yet figured out how to get the cuffs trimmed when the customer returned the following week. "Next week," they told the man. The following week, the pants still had not been tailored. "Forget it," the customer said. "Just give me my money back." Soon after, Morris and Elkin located a reliable tailor, but Elkin's son, current owner David Rubenstein, remembers ruefully, "The first suit they sold, they never sold."

The business ran on a narrow margin, and in the early years, each order of new merchandise nearly drained the shop's coffers. At one point, Morris and Elkin placed a C.O.D. order for polka-dotted ties — red, yellow, and green dots, on white silk, they assumed. When the order arrived, the brothers were appalled to find that the ties they had paid for were not in fact white, but an unfashionable shade of blue. The shipment coincided with a visit from the foppish Prince of Wales, whose fashion sense evidently carried a good deal of weight among young men at the time. Morris and Elkin, thinking quickly, hung a purely fraudulent sign in the window reading "Prince of Wales Blue Ties" and sold out the entire unwelcome inventory.

World War II dealt the business a compound blow: it drastically diminished the Rubenstein's male clientele, and the war effort's need for bandages commandeered most of the white fabric being manufactured stateside, halting supply of the store's best selling item — men's white shirts. When the war ended, the Rubenstein's were lucky to finagle through the Arrow company a large order of white shirts, which returning servicemen snapped up readily. The business prospered, and over the years, the store grew from its narrow boxcar shop on Canal Street to seven buildings, five on Canal Street and two on St. Charles. Today, Rubenstein's sells an array of men's casual and business attire from Ralph Lauren, Hugo Boss, Jack Victor, Canali, Zanella, and others, and has an expanded women's department as well.

In 1998, third-generation Rubenstein sisters, Allison and Hilary, opened up a young women's clothing store, ah-ha, at 3129 Magazine Street.

Waldhorn and Adler Antiques

343 ROYAL STREET

between Conti and Bienville Streets

MONDAY-SATURDAY 10AM-5PM

☎ 504-581-6379

SOCIAL REFORMERS AT THE END OF THE VICTORIAN ERA KNEW THERE WAS LITTLE HOPE THAT NEW ORLEANS WOULD EVER BE RID OF ITS THRIVING prostitution industry, but they thought it might at least be quarantined. In 1897, alderman Sidney Story proposed the nation's first legalized prostitution district, just north of the French Quarter—an area known, in wry tribute to the councilman, as "Storyville." As a reform tactic, Storyville was a catastrophe, but as a destination for prurient tourism, the district was a roaring success. Its taverns and houses of ill repute flourished, attracting vice seekers and merrymakers from across the globe, confirming New Orleans's reputation as the Babylon of the South.

(Storyville lent the city a more distinguished legacy as well: jazz came of age in the saloons and brothels of Basin Street. Jelly Roll Morton got his start playing piano in bordello parlors here, and King Oliver, Buddy Bolden, Kid Ory, Bunk Johnson, Sidney Bechet, and Louis "Big Eye" Nelson all played the Storyville circuit. A young Louis Armstrong got one of his first jobs in the neighborhood, carting coal to prostitutes' quarters.)

One of Storyville's busiest sporting palaces was the Arlington House at 225 Basin Street, owned by madam Josie Arlington. With its gaudy Hall of Mirrors, and Japanese, Turkish, and Viennese parlors, and a bar that served only imported champagne for $50 a bottle, the house was a tribute to garish luxury.

In contrast to the lush environs, Arlington herself was known as one of Storyville's more ferocious characters. An enthusiastic brawler in her trick-turning days, Arlington once bit off the ear and lower lip of a competitor. But Arlington had a gentler reputation where her employees were concerned. Early ledgers kept by Moise Waldhorn, one of the city's preeminent dealers of jewelry and antiques, chronicle annual Christmas-time purchases Josie Arlington made of rings and bracelets, gifts for her staff. Arlington was an unusual client for Waldhorn's Royal Street shop, which generally catered to the upper tiers of Southern aristocracy, but Waldhorn was an egalitarian businessman, and accepted the notorious madam's patronage gladly. Storyville was abolished in 1917, at the Federal Government's request, though Waldhorn's shop lived on.

Founded in 1881 in the wake of the Civil War, when many formerly wealthy Creole families were falling on hard times, Waldhorn's shop was known as "The People's Loan Office." Down-on-their-luck aristocrats, whose fortunes had dwindled to the family's store of jewels, stopped in on Waldhorn, who received them discreetly and gave them a fair price for their heirlooms. Following Waldhorn's death in 1910, the shop passed to his four children. Waldhorn's son Samuel ran it until his death in the early 1970s, when Moise Waldhorn's great-grandson, Stephen Moses, and Nancy Kittay took over the shop. In 1997, the local jewelry firm Adler's purchased the store and added its name to the sign.

Today, the store hosts three floors of French and English period furniture, both formal and provincial, and antique silver. The ground floor has a wide selection of antique and contemporary gold and precious-stone jewelry and watches by Rolex, Cartier, and Patek Philippe.

HOTELS

The Columns Hotel

3811 ST. CHARLES AVENUE

at Peniston Street

BAR HOURS FRIDAY-SATURDAY 3PM-2AM

SUNDAY-THURSDAY 3PM-12AM

☎ 504-899-9308

Years before Kate Chopin scandalized Victorian America with her novel *THE AWAKENING*, she was already ruffling feathers in New Orleans. Chopin, who in the 1870s lived with her family at 1414-1415 Louisiana Avenue, was a poor fit for Garden District society. She dressed scandalously, in flamboyant riding habits and plumed hats; she freely spoke her mind; and, most outrageously, she liked to smoke cigars—which, in the eyes of prudish uptown matrons, was a disgraceful thing to do.

Chopin's controversial stogies likely came from the warehouse of Simon Hernsheim, who was then the largest cigar importer in the United States. Hernsheim, with factories across the nation and overseas, had a house designed to reflect his successes—an imposing Italianate mansion on St. Charles Avenue. In September of 1883, the *Daily Picayune* reported that Hernsheim's new home would "equal or surpass any residence on the street," and that the cost of the mansion would exceed a staggering $40,000. But when Hernsheim's wife passed on and his daughter married a man Hernsheim didn't like, the magnate's wealth and stately home did little to ease his grief. In 1898, Hernsheim walked into his factory at 755 Magazine Street and swallowed a lethal dose of cyanide.

For nearly a century, the Hernsheim mansion was a respectable rooming house (It was named the Columns in 1953, obviously, for the huge Tuscan columns out front), though in the 1960s, the Columns fell into disrepair, as did many of the grand houses along St. Charles Avenue. When Claire and Jacques Creppel purchased the building in 1980, the years of neglect had taken their toll, and the Creppels undertook a massive renovation to restore its former elegance. The mansion's regal ballroom, which had been a shortwork of tenants' quarters, is now a beautiful hall with seven different species of marble and a pair of plaster ceiling medallions molded into an elaborate, swirling foliage. The hotel bar also underwent an impressive transformation. The drop ceilings were gutted to reveal a satiny expanse of coved and coffered mahogany. The lavish overabundance of dark wood, even at high noon, conveys an atmosphere of perpetual dusk. Late afternoon, in fact, is a good time to stop by for a drink, before the bar fills up with boozy parties of young professionals.

In the 1970s, the Columns portrayed a Storyville bordello in Louis Malle's film *Pretty Baby*, though the Columns is in fact one of the few old structures in New Orleans that has never housed a brothel.

Hotel Monteleone

214 ROYAL STREET

between Iberville and Bienville Streets

CAROUSEL BAR OPEN DAILY 11AM-2AM

☎ 504-523-3341 OR ☎ 800-535-9595

IN 1922, SHERWOOD ANDERSON CAME SOUTH TO NEW ORLEANS FROM OHIO, AND HE WAS PLEASED TO FIND A CITY THAT DIDN'T SEEM TO SHARE THE FRENZIED urgency he'd seen in the industrial North. New Orleanians preferred a slower, more expansive way of living, an attitude which, for Anderson, perfectly suited a literary life. In *The Double Dealer*, then the South's preeminent literary magazine, published from offices at 204 Baronne Street, Anderson wrote a sort of advertisement for New Orleans, beckoning other artists here:

"I address these fellows. I want to tell them of long quiet walks to be taken on the levee in back-of-town, where old ships, retired from service, thrust their masts up into the evening sky. On the streets here the crowds have a more leisurely stride . . . I stick to my pronouncement that culture means first of all the enjoyment of life, leisure and a sense of leisure. It means time for a play of the imagination over the facts of life, it means time and vitality to be serious about really serious things and a background of joy in life in which to refresh the tired spirits."

Writers answered Sherwood Anderson's call. William Faulkner, a great admirer of Anderson's, came to town in 1925 and moved into an apartment at 624 Orleans Alley (since renamed Pirate's Alley for tourists' benefit), where he would write his first novel, *Soldier's Pay*. Faulkner also wrote short sketches for *The Times-Picayune*'s Sunday magazine—backstreet anecdotes and literary snapshots of the French Quarter's hard-luck cases and menageries of grotesques—many of which later found their way into the pages of his novels.

Neither Faulkner nor Anderson took up permanent residence in New Orleans, but on return visits to the city, both stayed at the Hotel Monteleone on Royal Street. Over the years, the Monteleone has figured in the books of a host of authors, and in some of their personal mythologies as well. Truman Capote, for example, had a habit of telling people, "I came into this world in the Monteleone Hotel in the French Quarter in the grand old town of New Orleans"—a somewhat novelistic retelling of the facts. The author's mother did spend several days here, waiting in one of the hotel's suites for Truman to come to term. But when Truman's hour came, Lily Mae took a cab uptown to the Touro Infirmary to give birth. The hotel now has a suite named for Capote, and for other literary notables who have stayed here, among them Faulkner, Anderson, Tennessee Williams, and Eudora Welty, whose short story "The Purple Hat" includes a scene set at the Monteleone.

Sicilian cobbler Antonio Monteleone purchased the hotel in 1886, when it was a modestly furnished 64-room hotel called The Victor. Monteleone began adding rooms by the hundreds, and transformed the place with a small fortune in Italian marble and architectural embellishments. The hotel is now run by a fourth generation of Monteleones and is the French Quarter's oldest and most opulent hotel.

The Hunt Room Grill (dinner only) serves international cuisine with Creole tendencies. Entrees include grilled pompano with a lemon and parsley beurre noisette, Gulf shrimp Bienville, almond snapper, and grilled filet mignon served on fried eggplant with Burgundy-thyme sauce. The Aft-Deck Oyster Bar and Restaurant serves fresh-shucked oysters, jambalaya, stuffed seafood po' boys, gumbo, and crawfish pie. Tourists and well-to-do locals flock daily to the Carousel bar, whose piano was first played by Liberace in 1954. The bar's rear booths are quiet and confidential, but the best seats are at the revolving bar, which sits on a carousel engine and completes a slow, subtly intoxicating revolution every fifteen minutes.

Le Pavillon Hotel

O N A SWELTERING EVENING ON SUNDAY, SEPTEMBER 8, 1935, GOVERNOR HUEY LONG WAS WALKING WITH HIS ENTOURAGE THROUGH THE HALLWAY OF THE state Capitol in Baton Rouge when a man in a white linen suit approached the governor with a pistol in his hand. Long's colleague John Baptiste Fournet spotted the gun and, in a panic, swatted at the man with his hat. But the assassin, a man named Dr. Carl Weiss, sidestepped him and fired a single .32 caliber bullet into the governor's chest. "I'm shot," Long wailed and ran off down the hall. Long's bodyguards, who always followed the (rightfully) paranoid governor, unloaded a messy excess of pistol fire into Dr. Weiss, killing him on the spot. Long died Tuesday morning, September 10th, at Our Lady of the Lake hospital, still talking politics with his aides.

The fatal evening hadn't been the first time Long and Weiss had crossed paths. Months earlier, on July 21, a group of anti-Longites had gathered for a clandestine meeting at the DeSoto Hotel on Poydras Street to hatch a plot against Long, but the conspirators did a poor job of keeping the meeting secret. Long's camp got word ahead of time and hid a dictograph in the suite where the meeting was to take place (rooms 504, 505, and 506). "I would draw in a lottery to go out and kill Long," said an unidentified voice on the recording. "It would only take one man, one gun, and one bullet." Brandishing a copy of the dictograph transcript, Long accused the conspirators by name before a packed gallery. He had, however, deleted from the record a reference to "Dr. Wise," because, he said, he didn't want to ruin a man he didn't know. (Murder plots incidentally, were surprisingly common in Long-era politics. Long himself had been accused of planning a rival's assassination in 1929.)

In fact, the DeSoto conspiracy wasn't the first sinister bit of history to cast a shadow over this part of town. At the beginning of the nineteenth century, the land surrounding the hotel, then part of a suburb known as Faubourg St. Marie, had belonged to wealthy French planter Jean Gravier. He grew mostly sugar cane and indigo, which exuded poisonous fumes during fermentation and killed large numbers of the slaves who tended the vats. The late Judge Henry C. Castellanos wrote of this part of town that "no ordinary courage was required to venture alone within the precincts of that forbidding and dangerous spot.... With many it was associated with scenes of foul deeds and midnight murders."

By the turn of the twentieth century, the expanding grid of the Central Business District had civilized the former wilds of the Gravier Plantation, and in 1907 the New Denechaud Hotel, a palatial hotel, was built at the corner of Poydras and Baronne Streets. Not long after, the hotel changed hands and became the DeSoto. In 1970, under new ownership, the hotel underwent an radical restoration and was outfitted with extravagant furnishings—crystal chandeliers from Czechoslovakia, European marble flooring, and marble railings salvaged from the Grand Hotel in Paris—and was renamed Le Pavillon.

Alphabetical Index

Category Index

Restaurants

Neighborhood Index

NOTES

NOTES

Picture Credits

Cover Image: Vintage postcard of Old Absinthe House, collection of the publisher. Page 11: The Historic New Orleans Collection, accession no. 1989.84. La Belle Creole, ca. 1885. Page 39: Vestibule, French Market, New Orleans. Photo courtesy of Tulane University. Page 41: Old French Market. Photo courtesy of Tulane University. Page 79: The Historic New Orleans Collection, accession no. 1974.25.2.61. Bar of Old Absinthe House, Interior, ca. 1950-1973. Page 109: The Historic New Orleans Collection, accession no. 1979.89.7360. Roman Candy Wagon, ca. 1950s. Page 111: Photo courtesy of Rubenstein's. Page 112: September 26, 1949, at the Sazerac Bar. Photo courtesy of the Fairmont New Orleans. Page 121: Madame Begue in her kitchen. The Historic New Orleans Collection, accession no. 1981.261.32. Begue's Restaurant, Kitchen, ca. 1907. Page 133: Label courtesy of Bourbon French Parfums. Page 144: Stanley Herwig on a water bike on Lake Pontchartrain, 1933. Photo courtesy of Stanley Herwig. Page 147: Photograph courtesy of Keil's Antiques. Page 91: Anthony and Frank Mandina behind the bar at Mandina's, 1934. Photo courtesy of Mandina's. Page 150: Mendel Rau, ca. 1920s. Photo courtesy of M.S. Rau's. Obsolete labels on pages 10, 25, 89, 97, 125 are published under the registered trademark, Post Cards©, and cannot be duplicated without permission. Publisher: G2 Ltd. (800) 251-1006. Photographs on pages 17, 18, 22, 37, 42, 46, 53, 56, 63, 66, 70, 74, 79, 80, 84, 116, 122, 152, 161 © Angela Hederman. Vintage postcards on pages 28, 60, 94, 98, 130, 148 are from the collection of the publisher.

Acknowledgments:

The Little Bookroom would like to thank the owners of the establishments profiled in the book: Andrea Thornton, Mary Behler, Jim Miller, Andrew Ramsey, Anthony Tortorich, Anthony Uglesich, Bill Heim, Bill Johnston, Bobby Hennesy, Carrie Christian, Cary Alden, Chris "Bozo" Vodonavich, Coleman Adler, Collette Guste, Claire Creppel, John Dutton, Craig Napoli, David Rubenstein, Dot Domilise, Ernie Herwig, Evelyn Preuss, George Rapp Tranchina, Jr. & Sr., Glen Armantrout, Gunter Preuss, Ida Manheim, John and Sam Urrate, Jolie and Arthur Brocato, Jonette Franks, Jyl Benson, Kevin Tusa, Leah Deutch, Lloyd English, Mark Preuss, Mike Rodrigue, Nancy Kittay, Peter Moss, Keil Moss, Rick Rolland, Sal Impastato, Sam Meyer, Sandy Whann, Sasha Statman-Weil, Stephen Latter, Albert and Linda Mintz, Mitchell Mintz, Ti Martin, Tommy Mandina, Salvador Tusa, Bill Rau, Kit Wohl, Mark Radosta, Elizabeth Chopin.

The Little Bookroom would also like to thank for their efforts Borden Elniff, Matthew Jones, Cielo Lutino, Mario Pereira, Wells Tower, Lauren Wilcox, the staff of Lucullus, Sally Stassi at the New Orleans Historic Collection, William Meneray at Tulane University, and the New Orleans Public Library's Louisiana Collection.